To all those who have the courage to follow the way of initiation;
and to the ancestors, for their wisdom and help.

Acknowledgments

To Vivienne Hull, who reached out her hand as the Ancestors and helped me across the rope's course into new country. To my daughter, Elise, with much love and gratitude, for so graciously putting up with a mother with writer's brain.

To Gretchen Schodde for supporting me and my work so deeply and passionately. To the Silver Linings e-mail group for all your incredible love, support, and prayers. To Natasha Kern, agent extraordinaire, for your unflagging belief in this book.

To Alana Karran, Jean Frinak, Emma Bezy, Barbara Fischer, Diane Lachel, Beth Fischer, Debra Jarvis, and Lu Farber, sisters of my heart and soul. To the extraordinary people who make up the Harmony Hill community: staff, faculty, and retreat participants.

To all those who lent their immense wisdom, especially Barry Grundland, Jeanne Achterberg, David Spangler, Joseph Sharp, Jamal Rahman, and Barbara Fischer.

To Paula Munier at Fair Winds Press, for your unfailing enthusiasm for the book.

Contents

PART THREE: REBIRTH

Foreword

First, the bad news: Initiation is not an easy thing, although that's something you probably don't need to be told. Trauma has knocked me around that block now many times, through cancer, divorce, and relocation. I've had times, as I'm sure you've had, when I just didn't know if I was going to make it. As I wrote in my own chronicle of initiation, *Lightning at the Gate,* "When you are truly in the midst of a process that is so transformative that every cell in your being will shift, the future hides behind a brick wall. I figure if I did know the ultimate outcome, especially if it were really important to me or the world, I'd probably screw things up by rushing through some important steps, give myself a spiritual or psychological bypass in the process, and miss the whole point."

Now, the good news: The book you now hold in your hands will help you not rush through important steps. It will help you avoid the temptation of the quick fix of a spiritual or psychological bypass and open your heart and soul to the ultimate gifts your trauma has to offer you. *Silver Linings* is an astonishing guide to the power that trauma has to deeply transform and heal your life at every level.

Melissa and I met at a retreat I facilitated on cancer aftercare at Rancho La Puerta in Mexico. After a couple of days, we acknowledged each other as sisters with the same passionate mission: to share with those in trauma a map of the initiatory journey, and to let them know they have tools and resources to transform a shattered life into one of deep creativity and power.

Trauma sets up the necessary conditions for major transformation, which cannot and will not happen during the status quo. In the process of walking through the mystery, pain, and darkness, we have the opportunity to snatch the fire from the altar. During the flood of chemicals and sparks of electricity associated with stress, new neural connections are being formed; transmission of information across the synapses is sent with incredible speed. This condition, which utterly destabilizes us, results in an electrochemical cascade of opportunity to make new associations, to view the world in unique ways, and to have thoughts that have never occurred to us before.

Serious crises prime us for significant awakenings. Initiation invites us to wake up to a consciously lived life, both painful and ecstatic (we never get it just one way), a life naturally imbued with meaning and purpose. I haven't always felt that way. What I'm finding, though, in these successive initiations that life has offered me, is a growing and deeper trust in the wisdom of the process.

You can trust Melissa, and this book, as a guide for opening to and receiving this wisdom and new life. Blessings on your journey.

—Jeanne Achterberg, Ph.D.
Author of *Lightning at the Gate: A Visionary Journey of Healing*

Introduction

Welcome to the journey. Or rather, welcome to *your* journey. You may be in the midst of some trauma, or you may be a partner or friend of someone dealing with trauma. Your particular trauma—whether death, divorce, illness, betrayal, or some other form of terrible loss—may have happened yesterday, or it may have taken place ten years ago. Time doesn't matter to the psyche.

Trauma is terrible; there is simply no way around that. None of us would willingly choose it, myself included. However, trauma has another face, one that is rarely seen in our culture. Trauma carries the potential for tremendous healing and emotional and spiritual transformation. Those who consciously respond to trauma's invitation discover that a life of authenticity, joy, and even gratitude is forged from the terrible fire of their loss.

I came to this work through a series of traumas in my own life, a sort of on-the-job training: a promising musical career ruined by crippling tendinitis, life-threatening illness, divorce, and the recovered memories of childhood sexual abuse. Each was devastating, and each brought more fullness of life and depth of connection with Spirit in its wake.

In order to survive, I studied other cultures' rites of passage and traveled around the world with one question in my heart and mind: How can we work with devastation as a catalyst to new life? That question became my life's calling.

For the past twenty years, I have worked with hundreds of people in life transitions, as psychotherapist and spiritual director. I have worked with many more than that in workshops, retreats, and college classes on such topics as "Illness and Initiation" and "Broken Open, Not Down: Trauma as Invitation to New Life." I founded and directed LifeQuest, a nonprofit institute dedicated to contemporary life transition and ritual. I am currently Program Director for the Harmony Hill Retreat Center in Union, Washington, where I design curricula for psychospiritual retreats for people with life-threatening illness and their caregivers, and I help facilitate those same retreats.

I have lived and breathed this work for twenty years. I have watched people who have used this initiation map for navigating trauma step into larger, more passionately engaged lives. I'm honored now to be offering this map, and I'm deeply grateful for all those journeyers who helped create it.

There are several ways to work through the material in this book. You can read it cover to cover. You can, instead, locate where you are in the process, and begin reading there. Some of you may be guided to begin reading in a certain section for reasons that will gradually unfold to you. You will find Interludes at the end of each chapter in *Silver Linings*. These Interludes are exercises—journal keeping, guided meditation, art, and movement—that will help you ground the material of the preceding chapter and integrate it into your life. Some of us learn by doing. Others of us are more visual and learn from reading the chapters. You may also find, given how much internal energy it takes to move through an initiation, that on some days you have the interest and the energy to explore the exercises, while on other days you don't. *Any way you proceed with this book is fine; trust your instincts and your journey.*

Part One of Silver Linings, "Loss," takes you through the shock and grief of the first stage of the initiatory process triggered by trauma. Part Two, "Wilderness," is a guide to the betwixt-and-between time in the process, a time when your old life is irrevocably gone but you have not yet created your new life structure. Part Three, "Rebirth," helps you to name, claim, and celebrate your new life when it emerges.

The Chinese ideogram for crisis is composed of two smaller ideograms joined together: The first represents danger; the second, opportunity. This serves well as the ideogram for trauma. There is great danger in trauma, danger that a person might become permanently entombed in that pain or become addicted in some way to avoid it. You and I have all known people whose lives stopped at a moment of trauma and never began again.

But the opportunity is there, as well. Trauma's opportunity, the grace of misfortune, is the power to break us open to an ultimately deeper and richer life, rather than simply breaking us down. This grace of misfortune is yours to claim. May you work with the deep grief and pain of your suffering as a catalyst to your transformation and wholeness. My heart is with you on this journey.

PART ONE: LOSS

1
The Shattering

Has your life been shattered by trauma? Do you feel bruised and battered by illness or accident, violence or injustice? Do you feel disheartened, dis-spirited? Are you searching for meaning, asking, "Why me?" and "Why now?" If so, you are not alone.

But if you are struggling in the wake of trauma, you may feel very much alone. Trauma, in our culture, is seen as something to go through as quickly as possible. Those who become caught in trauma's grip may find themselves getting jollied, shunned, or guilted by others.

We have lost the real meaning and context of trauma.

From time immemorial, other cultures have seen trauma—with all its suffering, despair, and pain—as a sacred wounding, an opening through which all the love and assistance of heaven and earth could pour, a threshold to a powerfully open-hearted new life.

If you have picked up this book, chances are that you or a loved one are dealing with trauma. Perhaps you are in the midst of dealing with any of the following:

- Life-threatening illness in yourself or a loved one
- Grief over a "premature" or "senseless" death, such as the death of a child, a young partner, or a young parent

- Rape or other serious assault
- Traumatic divorce
- Serious accident or sudden disability
- Profound anxiety caused by the terrorist attacks of September 11, 2001
- "Hitting bottom" in an addiction cycle
- The recovery of old memories of physical or sexual abuse
- Fear and despair over our ailing culture, wholesale environmental destruction, and frightening global political instability
- Heart-breaking betrayal

If so, you are being given the opportunity, while reading this book, to ultimately experience your trauma as a catalyst to living a deeper and more meaningful life than you ever dreamed possible.

Listen now to this ancient story of the grace of misfortune.

You are in the desert, in the middle of this journey called your life. You stop for the night and go down to the river for a drink, lost in musing on how the next day's events will unfold.

Suddenly, a stranger leaps out of the darkness and knocks you to the ground.

You struggle to get up, only to find that he throws you back down. You muster all your strength and courage to push him away. Sand scratches your eyes and skin as you wrestle with this stranger. What does he want? Are you going to die? This assailant is relentless, and terrifyingly silent. You struggle hour after desperate hour in the darkness. This fighting for your life strips you to burning muscles and ragged breath. You can't fight on much longer.

And then something in you whispers, "Surrender." *Surrender?*

When you do, the struggle abruptly ends. He stands up, leaving you on hands and knees, heaving for breath. Pummeled and bruised, you clench the hem of his rough tunic in your hands. In the gray light of dawn, you look up into the eyes of this stranger: These are no human eyes. Their darkness and depth engulf you. Who is this? What Mystery has assailed you through this longest of nights? The stranger starts to pull away.

"No!" you gasp, "No! Who are you?"

This stranger looks down at you, through you, and you know at that moment that he is bigger than any name that could be uttered. He turns to go.

"No!" you cry once more. "I will not let you go unless you bless me."

Mystery looks into you a third time. Silently he reaches down and touches your thigh with his long, slender fingers, searing your muscle and shattering your bone.

This is a blessing?

Those eyes. This Mystery. The same hand that shattered your thigh now touches your head. Bliss floods your bruised body and soul, and it carries a message: "You have a new name and a new life. This is not the end of your life, though it may feel that way. This is your birth: you will go forth and beget nations. . . ."

He turns and disappears into the lonely stretch of desert and the river.

You stagger to your feet, deeply wounded, no longer the same person who came here to draw water in what seems an eternity ago. You will have a limp for the rest of your days. And yet, something within you knows that you are also deeply graced. You will now have a new name, a new life, and a new story to live.

The wound and the blessing both issued from the same hand of Mystery.

WRESTLING WITH THE ANGEL

Many of us grew up with this ancient Judeo-Christian story of Jacob wrestling with the angel. As a child I read it with curiosity—*What would it be like to fight with an angel?*—but then I outgrew the wonder of it.

It is only now, forty years later, that I can read this story with true understanding, having wrestled through many long nights with this angel. Some might say that one of his names is "Trauma."

In each of my encounters with the angel, my life as I had known it ended. Each experience of trauma stripped me of the comfortable and cozy assumptions I had woven around me—assumptions about myself, about how life worked, and even about who God was. I was shattered down to the very foundation of my soul. This is the experience of the first stage of initiation, a sense of being assaulted by larger and more powerful forces and being ripped away from what is known and familiar. In tribal cultures, such forces were understood to be sacred, working for the ultimate healing and transformation not just of the initiate, but of his or her community as well. In our culture, bereft of such knowledge, we experience these forces as alien and hostile to our very survival.

I wish that during the softer times in life—a week's vacation, watching a sunset, cradling a sleepy baby—we could wake up and ask ourselves some really important questions. What have I accumulated—beliefs, identities, relationships, habits—that is obstructing my essential and authentic self? How can I create a life in which the astonishing Light that is within me can blaze forth? How have I contracted, given away my power, resigned myself to smallness, settled for stumbling through my life, instead of opening to the great glory of life itself, of Spirit calling me to be who I truly am?

The truth is that most of us—myself included!—overlook or ignore the opportunities life offers us to stop and make major corrections in our life trajectories. We are like Bilbo Baggins in *The Hobbit*, secure and comfortable, unwilling to begin an initiatory journey that will utterly and forever change us. When a white-bearded wizard shows up at Bilbo Baggins' door with an "invitation," Bilbo tells the wizard Gandalf that he has no use for adventures: "Nasty disturbing uncomfortable things. I can't see what anybody sees in them." Caught up in the routine of our daily lives, we respond like Bilbo to the softer calls to wake up: No *thank* you! I like my comfortable chair, I like my afternoon tea, please go away and ask someone else. *Don't bother me.*

I don't live in Hobbit land, but I have often had the sense that life is calling me to greater adventures—and yet I refuse to respond. In more contemporary terms, it is as if I'm yakking on the phone and hear the beep of another call coming in. I'm so immersed in whatever I'm talking about that I don't press Flash to find out Who it is.

The beep comes again. Annoyed, I switch over to the other line and ask, "Who is it?"

"It's God," says the Voice.

"Oh, hi, God, can I put You on hold? I'm on this really important call."

I put God on hold and forget about that Voice waiting to speak with me. Several phone conversations later, the beep comes again. I guiltily remember that God called, press Flash, and find God once more on the other line.

"Oh, God, I forgot! Listen, is there a time I could call You back? I'm in the middle of this really important conversation. . . ."

Just before drifting off to sleep, I remember I didn't call God back, but figure there's always tomorrow. . . .

Trauma forces us to stop—not by choice, but through utter necessity—and behold our shattered life in shards around our feet. It seems only then that we can muster the courage to ask the Big Questions, listen to the voice of Spirit, and allow ourselves to be initiated into a larger, more heartfelt life.

STORIES FROM THE SHATTERED

I never would have chosen cancer—never in a million years—but I wouldn't trade what I've learned about myself and about the best way for me to live for anything, says Marge of her experience of being diagnosed with breast cancer four years ago.

My dream—always, always—was to have a happy marriage and a good home, recalls Jason. *When Marcia told me one weekend she wanted out of our marriage to be with one of my friends, it was like the sky fell in. My life ended. I was lucky enough to find someone to work with for a couple of years who helped me see that this could be a door and not a wall. It took everything to do it, but I walked right through that door. And I'm a different man today for it. I'm living a bigger life that I ever thought I could have. I'm doing things I've always dreamed about doing but never had the courage to do before. But I had to go through that awful door to get here.*

The rape was the worst thing I could ever have imagined, says Cynthia. *It was beyond anything I could describe. It took hard, hard work to move through it. But now, on the other side, I'm amazed at how much more alive and free I am than before the rape. It doesn't make sense, but it's true.* Cynthia worked with me for two years, taking it on faith that what I told her—that a new and more deeply authentic life awaited her on the other side of this trauma—was true.

Saul: *I still don't go a day without thinking about Hannah. She died three years ago; broke my heart in a million pieces. I didn't think I'd ever want to live again. We'd just been married six years—she was so young. Well, I still miss her, but it's strange: her death opened me up to living like I never thought I could. It's like her death gave me the gift of life.* Saul still misses his wife, but says he's never felt so alive in all his thirty-five years.

How can cancer be a *gift* to someone? How can traumatic divorce be a doorway into new passion and freedom? How can the agonizing premature death of a loved one be an invitation to new life? Why is it that—despite the terrible suffering and pain—these people say they wouldn't trade the lessons learned, the wisdom gained, and the new open-heartedness and full embrace of living for anything?

What if your loss were richly pregnant with meaning, not utterly devoid of it? What if your trauma were a "destiny point," a crucial window of time when it was possible to break free of old limiting beliefs, ruts, and life structures, and begin life anew? What if your trauma consecrated you as an initiate on a journey of radical awakening and transformation?

You, too, can move beyond our culture's denial of the soul-shattering and life-bestowing process of trauma. As you learn more about and move through the three stages of initiation—Loss, Wilderness, and Rebirth—you will join a lineage of initiates that winds back, unbroken, to the beginning of human history. You will partake of the wisdom and profound healing inherent in this process, and recover a deeper, wiser, more compassionate and more intensely alive self than you ever dreamed possible.

INITIATION

Trauma is an initiation.

Initiation, from the Latin *in ire*, means "a going into." Initiation invites us—no, requires us—to enter into grief, Mystery, and Big Questions to ultimately find wisdom and the holy ground of new life. Trauma initiates a quest for meaning, healing, and wholeness. We step forth—like Bilbo Baggins in

The Hobbit—on an initiatory journey to reclaim that which is missing in our life. Given our resistance to change, our fear of the unknown, and our comfort with what is secure and habitual, it's no wonder that most of us would never willingly choose initiation in the guise of trauma and loss.

As an initiate you are broken wide open, stripped down to the very ground of your being, looking directly into the dark and fathomless face of Mystery. All bets are off. Your old ways—the conditioned beliefs, assumptions, and surface appearances upon which your life was comfortably based—are burning to ashes in the fire of suffering. This burning, this breaking open to a larger reality, ultimately gives you new life and a new story.

In traditional cultures, periodic initiation was seen as a necessary part of the life cycle, a time when people released their old identities and "died" to their old lives so that they might be "reborn" into richer and fuller new ones.

"Initiation means change inside and out, not a simple adaptation or switch in 'lifestyle,'" writes Michael Meade, a mythologist and proponent of contemporary initiations, in his introduction to *Rites and Symbols of Initiation*. "Initiation includes death and rebirth, a radical altering of a person's 'mode of being;' a shattering and shaking all the way to the ground of the soul. The initiate becomes as another person: more fully in life emotionally and more spiritually aware."

I learned about initiation in the school of life, as we all do, through a series of traumas I suffered as a young adult. My first initiation occurred when tendinitis crippled my promising career as a pianist. My life as I knew it ended the morning the pain in my hands and arms was so severe that I could not turn my bedroom doorknob to open the door. I lost my profession, my dreams, my almost-completed graduate degree, my community of other musicians, and my innocence about how I thought life was "supposed" to be.

At age twenty-four, I had no knowledge of the process through which you will be led in this book. The tendinitis felt like a cruel joke randomly delivered by a meaningless universe. I wanted nothing to do with a God that could allow such haphazard cruelty. I floundered, depressed and dis-spirited, for several years until an old dream of being a therapist resurfaced.

Walking into the classroom on the first day of graduate-school therapy training, I knew that I had found my real vocation. As nervous as I was, my heart and soul thrummed with joy. Driving home that first day, I had a sudden realization at a stop sign. *Wait! I wouldn't be here, doing what I really want to do, if I hadn't suffered through the loss of my musical career.* I wanted to get out of the car and two-step with the old man reading a newspaper at the bus stop, but I restrained myself. *Maybe there was meaning in all that pain and despair.*

I pulled over to the curb to follow my thoughts. I remembered how being in such pain had driven me, relentlessly, to wonder why I was here and what I was supposed to be doing in my life. I recalled feeling like a teenager, ashamed to be asking such Big Questions—Who am I? Why am I here? I remembered feeling pursued by the pain and the questions until I had the courage to really look at my life and reclaim my childhood dream of helping others. I realized that, without the trauma of the tendinitis, I would still be at the piano, loving to play but feeling that something vitally important was missing from my life—a feeling I hadn't been willing to admit when I was a musician. This sudden realization ignited my training as a therapist. I became an explorer in trauma's rocky terrain, and began to notice that people generally responded to trauma in one of two ways. Some people—like the men and women you will meet in this book—allowed trauma to break their hearts and souls wide open not only to suffering, but to Mystery and the Sacred. This experience of being broken open ultimately led them to larger, more whole-hearted lives. The other group of people resisted the process. They contracted instead, pushing pain away, denying it, fighting it, or collapsing into victimhood. *Their trauma became a tomb rather than a birth canal.*

The angel of trauma visited me a second time some years later, when I began suffering flashbacks of childhood sexual abuse. The pain of betrayal and violation seared me like no pain I had ever felt. I did bodywork, I did talk therapy, I read self-help books and attended workshops. These lessened the pain, but did nothing to assuage an awful sense of disorientation, a feeling as if I had been dragged, unwillingly, into a new life and new sense of self. I struggled to get back to "normal," only to discover that there was now no "normal" to which to return.

I was driven to look beyond the way our culture psychologized and neuroticized the suffering of trauma. I began to get a wider perspective on how our culture dealt with—or didn't deal with—the kind of trauma and pain that turned a life inside out and upside down. I studied how other cultures dealt with such profound life transitions and discovered rites of passage and initiations. For several years I immersed myself in learning about how tribal cultures have recognized a universal three-stage process involved in profound turning points, and how they have created models for guiding people successfully through the metaphorical death and rebirth cycle. I recognized after years of work that the intractable pain of recovered memories of sexual abuse had marked me as a contemporary initiate. I understood, looking back on my healing, that I had undergone the same three stages of initiation—Loss, Wilderness, and New Life—that all tribal initiates underwent.

When I had grown self-assured and comfortable as a wife, mother, and successful psychotherapist, the angel visited me a third time. I became seriously ill with chronic fatigue immunodeficiency syndrome and fibromyalgia, losing two years to bottomless exhaustion and muscle pain, not knowing if I would ever get better, or if I would even survive.

This time, though, the pain and suffering had a meaningful context: initiation. I entered the process you will learn in this book, created a healing team, and asked myself the Big Questions once again: Who am I, really? What am I doing here? What can this illness teach me? Where am I being called to go, and with whom? I explored the Wilderness of my journey for several years, and finally moved into New Life. I was divorced now and had a new calling: to help others honor their trauma as powerful and ultimately life-bestowing initiations.

I began working with my clients and students as "initiates," and found that it greatly enhanced the healing work I did. Clients with whom I shared this material had a new context in which to see their pain. It didn't take the pain away, but it gave their pain meaning. I shared with them the map of the process that you will receive in this book. And, most important of all, I gave them reason to hope that New Life could arise from the ashes of the old. Michael Meade writes, "Learning the language of initiation means finding in the inevitable struggles of our own life certain types of real ordeals, the spiritual crises, the solitude and despair through which every human being must pass in order to attain to a responsible, genuine, and creative life."

I loved this reclaiming of the power of initiation for our times. I founded a nonprofit institute dedicated to educating others about contemporary initiations, taught medical students and health professionals about illness as an initiation, trained therapists to work with trauma as an initiatory process, and created curricula and led retreats for people with cancer and other life-threatening illnesses, as Program Director of the Harmony Hill Retreat Center.

From this vantage point twelve years out from my third initiation in the form of physical illness, I am unabashedly grateful for trauma's three shatterings of my life. During those awful times of being pinned down, struggling to survive, I could not see the Big Picture unfolding: transformation, healing, radical grace and new life in the aftermath of such great suffering. I would never have willingly invited that angel to touch me and metaphorically shatter my thigh. I now walk with a certain "limp" from these wounds, but these same wounds have been an aperture through which the light of grace has streamed into my life. Each of these encounters with Mystery brought "death": the end of a way of life and of my own identity as I had known it. Each of these shatterings, though, ultimately brought New Life: a more authentic self, new gifts and vocations, deepened intimacy with others and with Spirit, and a heightened ability to passionately dance with life, no matter what music the hidden band plays.

THE PROCESS OF INITIATION

Initiations in indigenous cultures permanently marked a person, like Jacob being forever wounded by the angel. And like Jacob's encounter, initiation also permanently blessed a person. Initiation always included ordeals that pushed a person beyond any previously held beliefs and limitations. One Aleut shaman described his initiation, during which he was left for a month in a tiny igloo just big enough to sit in. He recalled, "I died a number of times during those thirty days, but I learned and found what can be found and learned only in the silence, away from the multitudes, in the depths. I heard the voice of nature itself speak to me . . . and what it said was, 'Do not be afraid of the universe.'" In the article "The Great Initiation," historian Richard Tarnas writes that this discovery "became a point of internal, absolute security . . . and made possible his return to the community with a wisdom and assurance that was unmatched by everyone there, so that he could help others from that inner place" *(Noetic Sciences Review, Winter 1998).*

Tribal initiations were carefully constructed to trigger an experience of death and rebirth, which forced a paradigm shift in the initiate's worldview and consciousness. Through ordeals, ritual, and the guidance of elders, the initiate was reconnected to the center of creation and underwent a profound experience of spiritual awakening. The initiate released his or her limited and fragmented self and was opened to a greater identity and sense of place in the world. The initiate then brought the new wisdom and gifts back to the community.

Our brilliantly technological twenty-first-century culture has lost something essential for authentic living: the wisdom, power, and expanded heart and mind birthed from consciously experienced initiations. We have forgotten that we must go through the deep pain of metaphorical death in order to experience the great gifts of rebirth. We have lost the old rites of initiation. We have privatized and psychologized trauma, robbing pain of its transformational power.

Like tribal initiations, contemporary trauma has three stages:

• **Loss.** The death of the old life. This may occur suddenly—an accident, a medical diagnosis, the shock of sudden betrayal. The loss may also occur over an agonizing stretch of time—a marriage painfully unraveling in separation and divorce, or watching a loved one suffer a painful decline and death from terminal illness.

• **Wilderness.** An extended period of questioning and turning within, a tremendously creative time "betwixt and between" the loss of the old life and the birth of the new. I call it Wilderness because it is unknown and unexplored territory, and because Wilderness is where mythical heroes and heroines often journeyed to receive spiritual guidance and new direction.

• **New Life.** The gaining of wisdom and a powerfully open-hearted new life. For some people, New Life may blossom forth wildly and suddenly. For most of us, it occurs gradually and imperceptibly, like the first shoots of spring bulbs showing green through frozen ground.

As an "initiate," you will undergo the same universal challenges a tribal initiate undergoes in each stage. Like a tribal initiate, you will never return to "normal," to your pretrauma life. The final stage of your initiation, New Life, is just that: moving into a new life structure deeply informed by the "radical altering of your mode of being," as Meade writes. Just like a tribal initiate, you will emerge with new wisdom and gifts to be used to bring new life and hope to our ailing culture.

Joseph Sharp, author of *Living Our Dying*, was diagnosed with AIDS at age twenty-one. Suddenly uprooted from a life where "he who gets the most toys wins," Sharp ultimately found a new vocation as a hospice chaplain, after many years of soul searching:

> *My personal and professional experience with trauma has taught me that whether you like it or not, trauma is an initiation. You don't really have a choice about that. Now as to whether or not you want to be aware of the initiation and learn the lessons of the initiation, whether or not you want to be an active participant in it, that is your choice. Life is initiating you into lessons whether you decide to be aware of them or not. We're all given unique gifts to offer the world. Within your particular trauma there are things that are just yours, your lessons. It's your life it's happening to, so use it. Let it affect you. Let in the grit of your trauma, and recognize that there is a grace of initiation going on.*

It is our *response* to trauma that makes all the difference. Trauma enlarges us when we work with it as an initiation; it diminishes us if we refuse its gifts.

When we recognize our life traumas as initiations, we can:

- Tap into a body of knowledge and experience about initiation that is as old as humankind
- Receive a "map of the territory" of its predictable stages and challenges
- Receive the gifts and wisdom that are ours as "initiates"
- Experience deep emotional healing and a radical opening of the heart
- Undergo accelerated spiritual awakening
- Gain the capacity to trust and wholeheartedly embrace life

After a successful initiation, we are in new country. We carry with us the limp (even if it just shows up on bad days), a new identity, and a new story to live. The old frames of reference, the old limiting beliefs and ways of life, are gone, never again to return.

Initiations take time and consciousness, neither of which our culture grants us. We'll miss the opportunity of initiation if we behold trauma through our cultural lens as something awful to be gone through as quickly as possible in order to "return to normal." We can reclaim both time and consciousness and gather support around us for moving through such profound life events as initiations. We can learn to compassionately honor ourselves as the initiates we truly are, and thereby receive the precious and life-changing gifts from the process of initiation.

"Tell me: what is it that you plan to do with your one wild and precious life?" asks poet Mary Oliver. I invite you to move with me into *Silver Linings: The Power of Trauma to Transform Your Life*. Know that as you read, you join a great community of initiates that stretches back through time for thousands of years and reaches all around the world. Let us begin.

Interlude One

You will find Interludes such as this one at the end of each chapter. The interludes include exercises to ground and deepen the material of the foregoing chapter. If you wish, and if you have the energy and time, play with these Interludes. You may do them in the order presented, pick and choose from among them, read them but not do them, or simply skip them altogether. (That's why I call them Interludes.)

I have wasted far too much of my own life energy feeling guilty about not doing exercises in self-help books. I have gathered ingredients for the recommended projects, only to stash them in the back of the closet "for extra insulation," as a friend once said. I have bought notebooks that I have finally slid under the couch into oblivion, reproached by their silent emptiness.

That being said, I still received enormous help and hope at times from these same books, without "doing" anything. At other times in my life, when I have had the energy and inclination, I have done the exercises and projects recommended in books and benefited enormously.

So take these exercises (or not) at your own pace. For some of you, these may be a lifeline and a Godsend. For others, just getting through the day is enough. Trust yourself and what you know you need.

INITIATION JOURNAL

Find a three-ring binder in a color you like, or a large spiral hardcover sketchbook. This will be your initiation chronicle, a record of your journey. Divide the journal into five sections: Journey, Dreams, Gratitudes, Questions, and Quotes. Use section dividers for a binder, or glue paper tabs onto pages of a sketchbook. Make the first section, "Journey," the largest; the next section,

"Dreams," the next largest; then "Gratitude" the third largest, and the two final sections much smaller. "Journey" is your journal, your place to vent, to be thoughtful, to reflect whatever mood and frame of mind you're in; this section will be a clear mirror for your heart and soul.

"Dreams" is a place to record your night dreams, which—as you will see in Chapter Eight—may be vivid during this initiation journey. These dreams will serve as both compass and guide. If you wish, you may skip ahead to Chapter Eight and read about recording and working with dreams. For now, though, it is enough to simply create the section and, when you remember a dream in the morning, record it, dated, in the present tense. Leave the back of the page blank to write further thoughts on the dream.

"Gratitudes" is a place for articulating what you are grateful for. In the first part of the initiation process, enumerating what you are grateful for may feel like a mockery of your pain. Don't start until you're ready. Chapter Nine and Interlude Nine will offer instructions on how to use this section to open your heart and deepen your spiritual journey.

"Questions" is a section for you to record just that: questions. It is also your space to play with answers, as well. Our ability to ask questions often slides underground after adolescence. Adults, after all, are the ones who know all the answers; it's kids who ask silly questions (Why is the sky blue?), and adolescents who ask searching questions (What is the meaning of life? Why am I here? Who is God? Is there a God?).

Initiation is your opportunity to reclaim that wondering, questioning, questing part of yourself. Poets and sages throughout time have reminded us that simply asking the question is important: It opens a space inside of our hearts and souls for wonder, for not-knowing, for Mystery. These same wise ones tell us that it is ultimately more important to love and live into the questions than to contract into a demand for answers. They assure us that if we have the patience to learn to love the questions, they will ultimately be answered in deeper, wiser, more truthful ways than we could create ourselves.

Record all your questions, from the most patently unspiritual (this is one I excel at, written in a very whiny voice: "This isn't fair; why me?") to the Big Questions about the nature of life, God, and yourself. Don't edit. All questions (even the whiny ones) contain a nugget of wisdom waiting to be revealed. This is a place to simply state your questions and let them be. If you want to do more with them, you may look ahead to Chapter Eight.

Finally, "Quotes" is a place for you to record from this book and any other sources quotations that inspire and support you on this journey. Poetry, something you overheard while standing in a checkout line, your grandmother's favorite saying, and spiritual aphorisms all have a place in this section. I still refer back to the quotations I have collected during journeying times; they continue to inspire me today.

When you take time to write in your journal, make sure you are going to be uninterrupted for the duration. Turn off the phone, close the door, let the kids or your partner know you're off-limits for a little while. I often find it helpful to light a candle (to remind me of the presence of Spirit, and my own inner divine flame) and say a prayer for guidance and support in telling the truth to myself. Doing this marks the time for myself, alone with my journal, as sacred. Experiment with ways to symbolize for yourself that this is time set apart for yourself. Give yourself the freedom to simply open your journal and vent, or plunge into question asking. There is no right or wrong in the process; it is simply you calling yourself Home.

2
The Leaving

"When Marcia walked out that door, the world ended," recalls Jason about the rainy spring night his wife left him. "Oh, yeah, I know I'm supposed to say *my* world ended, but that wasn't true. It's like *everything* ended. Those couple of months after she left, it was like I was in a dream. I watched everyone else doing normal things—chatting at work, standing in grocery lines, jogging—but it was like they were on another planet, and I was somehow in a parallel universe. I felt like an alien. During that time, my world really had ended when she slammed the front door shut."

THE END IS WHERE WE START FROM

Trauma ejects us, uncomprehending, from our known world, mercilessly tearing away all that is familiar, comfortable, and known. Like Jason, we feel that the world as we have known it ends.

The poet T. S. Eliot, in his immense wisdom, echoes what sages and tribal elders have known all along:

What we call the beginning is often the end
And to make an end is to make a beginning.
The end is where we start from.

We normally think of birth as the beginning and death as the end. But initiation and deep transformation of the psyche turn everyday thinking on its head: Initiation always begins with a death and ends with birth. Those wise in the ways of the birth-death cycle and nonlinear time insist that the story always begins with endings: Hansel and Gretel evicted from their childhood home. The Buddha renouncing princedom and the glittering enclaves of the only home he had ever known. Persephone roughly abducted into the Underworld.

Jason: "A friend said to me, 'Jason, look at the bright side of things. You're free! You can do whatever you want! You're rid of a bad marriage—celebrate!' I *know* it was a hard marriage, but, dammit, it's what I knew. You don't just shrug off fifteen years of marriage. It was the end of a lot of hopes and dreams. It was the end of my future: Marcia and me with white hair, holding hands and strolling through the neighborhood in the evening. It was the end of being a 'married person.' It was the end of sharing my life with someone who had known me since I was twenty. It was like she took away that time of my life when she left, a time when none of the friends I have today knew me."

The end is where we start from.

Your ending—shattered relationship; diseased heart, liver, or breast; death of a partner, parent, or child—is actually an initiation, a beginning. Mircea Eliade, a lifelong scholar of initiation, once wrote, "In no rite or myth do we find the initiatory death as something final, but always as a trial indispensable to regeneration; that is, to the beginning of a new life."

Initiations are seldom welcome, however, even as harbingers of new life. In my twenty years of working with people in trauma, not one, in the first stage, has *ever* felt any gratitude or excitement about the initiation process. My response to the "initiations" I've undergone since becoming aware of this process—recovery of sexual abuse memories, serious illness, divorce, and my dearest friend's struggle with cancer—has been the same. Even with years of working with hundreds of people as initiates, my response to personal trauma, in this first stage, has been the same as everyone else's: This is awful. This is unfair. I hate this. Why me?

THE BIG PICTURE

Two different perspectives on trauma exist, and both are "real."

Imagine being lost in a dense forest. All you can see is close-set trees. Very little light filters in from above. The ground-level view of trauma is that it is terrible. *And it is terrible.* Such a close-up perspective means we can see only what is immediately visible: the loss, the pain and suffering. This view is usually the only one accessible at the beginning of trauma.

Imagine now what an eagle, circling in a thermal high above that dense patch of woods, might see. To the eagle, the thick stand of trees would be visible, but only as part of a much larger "reality" of meadows, forests, sky, and light. What seems like an endless forest at ground level would appear to the eagle as a small piece of a much larger terrain. From his airborne advantage, the eagle can see the Big Picture.

In the same way, the Big Picture of trauma is a radically different perspective. It sees the experience of trauma as the first stage of a larger process that utterly transforms a person. It sees loss as a death, but a death that, if honored, can be a catalyst to a larger and freer life, a wiser and more deeply spiritual life. The Big Picture sees Loss as an invitation to deeper soulfulness, and a harbinger of wisdom.

How you "see" your trauma will deeply affect your journey through it. You can allow yourself to be victimized by your loss and spend the rest of your life contracted in pain, anger, bitterness, or remorse. We've all met people who entombed themselves with the death of a spouse or the loss of a cherished dream. You can also choose, as Joseph Sharp counseled in the first chapter, to take the terrible grit of your trauma and allow it to become a catalyst for emotional and spiritual healing.

This doesn't mean that when trauma eviscerates your life, you should fall down on your knees and thank God for this amazing opportunity. *Trauma never initially feels like a gift.* What is most important at first is to allow yourself to feel the pain during this time and get support for your grief. As you enter the second stage of the initiation process, holding the Big Picture—and, most important, finding someone who holds it for you when you feel that you can't—will enable you to access help and power that would be unavailable from a standpoint of victim consciousness. This doesn't mean that you won't feel victimized from time to time. What it does mean is that you won't linger there any longer than necessary. Understanding your trauma as the beginning of a powerful initiatory process allows you to be an active participant in your own journey, seeing this time as a catalyst for a more deeply lived and heartfelt life.

Tribal cultures, embedded in the great cycles of life, death, and rebirth in nature, were able to hold initiation in this larger context. They celebrated the cycles of the seasons, knowing that the bleakness of winter always yielded to the green exuberance of spring. Gazing skyward, they watched the moon die monthly, but knew it would be reborn, no matter how deep the darkness.

Gretchen, my dearest friend and a passionate gardener, was diagnosed with cancer one fall. As the grueling course of chemotherapy began, she consciously participated in winter—when all signs of visible life drop away—both literally and metaphorically. Having grown up on a farm and gardened through countless cycles of the seasons, Gretchen knew "in her bones" that spring, rebirth, always follows winter. Through a long winter of chemotherapy, nausea, hair loss, suffering, and an intense reordering of her life priorities, Gretchen kept reminding herself that even though she was in the depths of winter, spring would come. There were days for her when it was hard to believe, just as there are dreary January days in the Northwest when it feels as if the rest of life will be nothing but a succession of dark and rainy days. Spring did come, as did the end of her chemotherapy, and with it came a clean CT scan of her lymph nodes.

We have become so divorced from nature's seasons and cycles that we have forgotten our place in these great rounds of life, death, and rebirth. For some of us, the winter of our initiatory process will last months, like Gretchen's; for others, that winter may last years. Our initiatory winter has its own rhythm and life; it is part of our healing journey to learn to honor that, and not to try to force spring.

INTANGIBLE LOSSES

Loss, the first stage of the initiatory process, represents not only the physical loss we are mourning—a relationship, our health, or our vocation—but intangibles as well. These intangibles—hopes, dreams, and cherished beliefs—are embedded in the physical loss, and are often the most painful aspect of the loss, even though they may be unconscious and unnamed. William Bridges, in his wonderful book *Transitions*, enumerates four invisible aspects of Loss: Disengagement, Disidentification, Disenchantment (or, as I call it, Disillusionment), and Disorientation. I have, in my own life and in my work with others, found a fifth "dis": Disintegration.

When I first read Bridges' descriptions of these intangibles—in the "winter" of my own serious illness—I felt intrigued, as a writer, by the prefix "dis" heading up each of the categories. One afternoon when I wasn't totally incapacitated by the profound exhaustion of chronic fatigue syndrome, I looked up the origins of "dis." To my great surprise, lying there on my couch in the waning afternoon sunlight, I found that "Dis" was another name for Pluto, the Roman God of the Underworld. The word "dis," I continued to read, was derived from the Latin word for wealthy. Romans believed that the Underworld was the ultimate source of wealth; although dark and terrifying, rubies, riches, and gold all issued from its mysterious depths.

I was stunned. Yes, I was in the Underworld. I was too ill some days to do more than get dressed. I felt depressed and in despair of ever getting better. I didn't know if I'd run again, or even walk around the block. I was too tired to even read books, once one of my greatest pleasures. My world had narrowed to the four walls of my house.

Here, though, was hope: This same Underworld in which I dwelt was also considered the source of the greatest riches imaginable. Perhaps Bridges' "dis" words were the same.

As you read about Disengagement, Disidentification, Disillusionment, Disorientation, and Disintegration, apply them to your own intangible losses. Unnamed, they eat away at your heart and soul, and the hidden wealth remains forever untapped. Once named, though, they can be mourned and then mined for their secret riches. If you were an initiate in a tribal culture, you would be deliberately subjected to this process. The tribal elders knew that being broken down, and broken open, by these intangible losses was requisite to new life, new vision, new gifts. For a contemporary initiate, the hidden riches will be unmineable at the beginning, and perhaps for a very long while. It would be cruel and useless to try to force an appreciation of them at this stage. It is enough for now, and deeply necessary, to simply name the losses.

Disengagement. If you were an initiate in a tribal culture, you would first be forcibly removed from your familiar context. You would be physically taken from your family, your traditional work, all that is known and comfortable, and placed in new and totally unfamiliar surroundings.

Chronic fatigue syndrome did this for me, just as your trauma is doing it for you. I remember going to the grocery store and feeling, as Jason did, that everyone else inhabited some parallel reality. I felt cut off from the known, the secure, the stable. The world in which I now dwelled—one of unremitting fatigue, painful muscles, doctors' visits, medication, and endless nights of exhausted insomnia—bore painfully little resemblance to the one I had once so taken for granted.

Marge remembers the moment she was ejected from her world. In shock from receiving her diagnosis of breast cancer, she left the doctor's office and discovered the world had changed. "The same trees were there, the same shops, the same traffic, but I had this awful feeling that I was in a totally different world. This world had different rules than the one I had left an hour ago. I burst into tears right there on the street. I wanted that old world back, but I knew it was gone."

Clients that I work with often come to sessions with dreams of not being able to find their home, of being lost or abducted. We are metaphorically abducted from the familiar "home" of our comfortable beliefs, relationships, identities, and way of life. We try to find that lost home in whatever way we can, but it is an impossible task: That home is gone forever.

Disidentification. At a tribal initiation, all distinguishing markers that identified you as "you" would be stripped away: Your head might be shaved, your name changed, your face and body painted until you were unrecognizable, your belongings burned. Elders would sever you from all reminders of yourself to create psychic space for your deeper and wiser self to emerge.

This same process happens in contemporary trauma. However, it is not the elders who take your "you-ness" away, but trauma. One of Jason's identifying markers had been the role of a married man. Without it, he told me, he felt like a boat that had been previously anchored in a safe and secure harbor, but whose ropes had been cut, casting it adrift on some unknown sea.

I understood what he meant as I recalled being cast adrift with chronic fatigue syndrome. I, who had always prided myself on my intellect, would now forget the beginning of a sentence before I came to its end. I, a gardener, hiker, runner, and world adventurer, now sometimes spent whole afternoons in a chair, too weak to do anything but watch the patterns of sunlight shift across the ceiling as evening approached. I used to be witty, sociable, and attractive; now I couldn't remember a punch line no matter how short the joke. I visibly aged. I remember sometimes staring at the mirror in utter incomprehension at this stranger I had become.

Disillusionment. Imagine your shock as a tribal initiate, when you were told that the gods who danced every year during the festivals were really your uncles, or shown that the sound of a god roaring at the rituals was really a simple musical instrument.

In our modern technological sophistication, we no longer have such "illusions" to release. We have, however, our own deeply cherished postmodern illusions instead: the illusions of control, safety, and security. We carry a lot of the world in our heads, and when outer circumstances change as a result of trauma, the world inside our head changes as well. We don't realize that the picture we carry in our heads of "the way life is supposed to be" is deeply at odds with the true circumstances of the world we live in.

Most of us believe, against all evidence, that if we are "enough" (as in rich enough, spiritual enough, powerful enough, or healthy enough), we will be spared loss, pain, suffering, and grief. With insurance, rigorous exercise, IRAs, and the healthy diet du jour, we carefully construct an illusion of having control over life's vicissitudes.

Jason realized several months after Marcia left him that he had always believed that being the best husband he could be would inoculate him from divorce and guarantee him his dream: a happily married life forever. I was shocked and outraged when I discovered that I had a life-threatening illness: How could it be true? I ran three miles a day. I ate healthfully. I went to therapy. I had a close group of loving friends. I had constructed a barrier between myself and possible or potential suffering that seemed thick and impenetrable. How could I get so sick when I had been so good? I helped others, I contributed money to worthwhile organizations, I prayed. I had held up my end of the bargain; where was God?

A seeker once asked a wise man what he considered to be the greatest mystery in human life. The wise man thought a moment and replied, "The greatest mystery is this: that a human being sees the sickness, pain, suffering, and ultimate death of others and thinks that he will be the only one spared."

Disorientation. Add up all the above losses, and the sum is one very disoriented individual. Just as sailors orient themselves by the North Star or travelers by the compass's true north, so we all carry a sense of "true north," a defining orientation in our bodies and souls. Life is "supposed" to be a certain way, relationships a certain way, and we navigate our lives unconsciously by these pole stars. When our compass needle begins to swing wildly, when a storm covers all traces of a guiding light in the sky, we get lost. How can we continue on when our partner or our child dies? How are we supposed to behave if we are no longer an attorney, a housewife, a parent, a healthy person? How do we neatly package ourselves for the outside world, where we are inevitably asked who we are and what we do, when we don't have a clue?

Once, in the depths of my illness, I decided a haircut would lift my flagging spirits. I called my hairdresser; he was out sick, and I was assigned a new one. As I drove to the appointment, I felt funny, but I didn't recognize my mounting panic until I parked and looked into the rearview mirror at myself. I was terrified to go spend an hour with someone I didn't know and chitchat about my life. At that moment, I felt as if I *had no life*. How could I hold myself tightly together for an hour and pretend I did? How could I stand looking at three different reflections of myself for an hour, when I didn't even recognize the "me" in those mirrors? I put the key back in the ignition, drove home, and canceled the appointment.

Disintegration. As a result of being so deeply affected by the "dis-es," we lose our previous integrity of self; we start to disintegrate emotionally. Our cherished beliefs and expectations and the life we once led lie around us in shattered pieces, mocking us in our confusion and grief.

Western culture sees adulthood as a plateau to be gained and maintained: When we finally earn enough money, get the right house and car, and find the right partner, we can sit back to enjoy the landscape. Instead of a valid road map for a fully engaged and soulful life, our culture hands us a pack of lies about the adult journey: If we just have the right belongings (whether material possessions or inner belongings such as an ironclad positive attitude or faith in God), then we will be forever rich and healthy. Pop psychology (remember *I'm OK, You're OK?*) feeds our need to believe that we can be perennially happy if we just do enough "inner child" work or participate in enough weekend workshops.

Tribal cultures and all deeply spiritual traditions assert instead that life is a series of disintegrations and subsequent reintegrations at a higher or deeper level. Victor Turner, an early anthropologist who spent a lifetime studying tribal initiations, once wrote, "All further growth requires the immolation of that which was fundamental to an earlier stage."

Bereft of that tribal map of initiation, we are also bereft of its wisdom, which teaches that initiations will happen to us all; that these initiations have a meaning and an ultimate teleological purpose; and that if trauma casts us adrift, like Jason, the Divine will carry us to a new shore.

One night in the midst of my time of dealing with childhood sexual abuse, I had this dream: *A great storm has come and destroyed my home, including all my childhood photo albums. In order to save myself, I run down to the dock, in the driving wind and rain, and leap into the boat there as my home collapses. The waves are high and frightening, and I am blown far into the water before I discover that the boat has neither oars nor rudder. Even though I know somewhere deep inside me that I am being carried to a new land, and a new home, I am terrified. I cannot even hear my own crying above the wind and the rain.*

You, too, have been cast adrift from the moorings of your old life. The deeper reality is that you are now being carried to New Life by the winds and currents of the Divine. In that boat, though, all you know right now is loss. The end is where you're starting from.

Interlude Two

JOURNAL KEEPING

Pick a time for working on your journal when you can be undisturbed. If you wish, light a candle before you begin, and say a prayer asking for support, wisdom, and guidance. Take out your Initiation Journal and turn to the first section, "Journey." We're going to focus on the "dis" aspects of your loss. *If this feels like too much right now, don't do it!* As you'll see in the next chapter, we all have different timetables for moving through grief and loss. Trust your own journey.

It is most important during this first stage to be compassionate and gentle with yourself in your pain. You can leave this exercise for another time when you're feeling stronger or, if you're in therapy or receiving spiritual direction, do this work in the presence of your compassionate guide. Go through the questions for each "dis" and answer with as little censorship as possible; allow yourself to be surprised by what may emerge. When you feel as if you've said it all, try switching your pen or pencil to your nondominant hand. Ask the same questions, and simply let your nondominant hand respond, bypassing your critical mind. Often our nondominant hand carries wisdom and insights that are simply not accessible to our dominant hand.

Disengagement. What are some aspects of your "old" world that you have left behind? What habits have you lost (for instance, morning coffee with a spouse now lost through divorce, or an evening walk around the block now impossible with illness)?

Disidentification. What self-images have you lost? What roles? What labels for how you identify yourself?

Disillusionment. What old beliefs and expectations of life have you lost? What bargains did you make with life, God, or yourself that have been broken? (If I do X, then life will give me Y.) What illusions of safety, security, and control have you lost? How is life no longer the way it is "supposed" to be?

Disorientation/Disintegration. Are there times you feel disoriented or disintegrated? How do you care for yourself when you feel this way? What else might you do for yourself in a compassionate way?

INITIATION ALTAR

An altar represents the meeting of heaven and earth, a physical space where we can honor the intersection of our life and the sacred, a place for personal devotions, prayer, and listening to divine guidance. A home altar, writes Denise Linn in *Altars*, "can assist the journey toward healing and self-integration, and help us find courage to face life's challenges."

We are altar makers by nature: a collection of family photos on the piano; a vase of flowers, a candle, and a seashell or beautiful stone on your bedside table. A conscious altar can be large and lavish: a tabletop with statues, a fountain, candles, crystals, and scarves. An altar can also be small and simple: a photo and flower on a windowsill, a small shelf with a tea light and tiny statue, an alcove in the wall with some water or earth from a holy place and a special stone, or even a shoebox on its side in a corner of your bedroom. The size and complexity are much less important than how the altar speaks to your heart and calls you back to Spirit.

Find a place in your home that feels private. This space will be important for your initiation journey. It will call you back to your deepest self, remind you of the presence of the Divine, and support your healing through various objects you may put in it from time to time.

If you wish, say a brief prayer for this space to be blessed as a healing altar for your journey. Depending upon its size and your needs, possibilities include:

- A pretty cloth or scarf to cover the shelf or space
- A candle (either full-size, or a small tea light)
- Icons of the sacred, such as photos, postcards, or drawings

- Favorite small stones or crystals
- Any object that feels grounding, healing, or special to you
- For grieving, a photo or symbol of what you've lost, or mementos from the past
- A favorite prayer, poem, or quote
- Flowers or a small plant
- Small statues of spiritual figures or animal allies
- An incense burner

When you've assembled your altar, light a candle or a stick of incense if you wish, and simply allow yourself to sit with it for as long as you're comfortable (a minute or two is fine). Say a prayer asking for Spirit to be with you in this journey, pray for healing or guidance, or simply sit in silence. Also know that your tears are a prayer; the altar is a wonderful place to bring your grief.

As you continue into your initiation journey, the objects on your altar may change as your needs change. You may rearrange it or add different elements and objects that speak to you at points in your journey. Personal altars are alive in some soulful way; they change as you change. Feel free to remove something when it no longer has significance to you. Feel free also to keep the altar exactly the same if that feels grounding to you at a time when you need it most. This altar is yours, to promote your own healing and to call you back to Spirit in your own way.

I will often spend just a minute or so in front of my altar, light a candle, and say a prayer for God to be with me during the day. I will ask for help in remembering my own heart, and the presence of God, in the midst of whatever else I have to do. If I'm going to be in the house, I will leave the candle burning as a way of honoring the Presence of the sacred in my life.

3
Loss and Heartbreak

Initiation breaks our hearts.

The good news is that a heart broken open is halfway to a radically spacious heart, a tender and compassionate heart, a heart of wisdom, a heart that has room enough for the whole world.

The bad news, as you know from experiencing your own trauma, is that a broken heart hurts, especially in the first weeks and months of raw grief. It hurts so much that you want more than anything to shut down and crawl into a hole for a very long time. It hurts enough to seriously question, at 3:00 A.M. of your sixth consecutive night (or month) of insomnia, whether life is worth living anymore.

Grief—even deep, searing grief—is a process and a journey. While you're deep in it, though, it feels more like a dead end, a brick wall behind which you'll take up permanent residence.

I remember learning Dr. Elisabeth Kubler-Ross's six stages of grief in graduate school: Denial, Anger, Bargaining, Depression, Acceptance, Hope. "Aha!" I thought with great satisfaction. "A clean, neat model I can use to help my future clients." I felt elated to know that, in the messy realms of the human psyche, there existed a model of order, which was a great solace to a graduate student terrified of wading into that mess.

Life in the ensuing years, however, showed me something altogether different. Trauma—both mine and others'—taught me that raw grief in the wake of trauma is neither linear nor orderly, but is instead an unpredictable melange of many different feelings. One day I would feel nothing, a numbed-out overload. The next day (or even the next hour!), the grief would crash over me in huge waves. I might stay there for hours or days, and then the grief might give rise to anger, or peace, or despair. "Grief, as I read somewhere once, is a lazy Susan," writes Annie Lamott in *Traveling Mercies*. "One day it is heavy and underwater, and the next day it spins and stops at loud and rageful, and the next day at wounded keening, and the next day numbness, silence."

So, I'll share with you the "lazy Susan" way through grief. It is most important to discover how you need to grieve and what best supports *you* in the process, rather than follow a cookbook approach to the "right" way. Please know: *There is no "right" or "wrong" way to do grief. There is just your way.*

"Grief is the most overpowering feeling imaginable; there are just no words to describe it," says Diane Nares, who lost her only child, Emilio, age five, to leukemia. "I asked myself, 'How does one breathe again?' At times it was even hard to breathe."

After trauma, it takes time to move through the early grief. The three most important tasks during this stage are giving the grief the time it takes, asking for support, and extending compassion to yourself as a mourner.

GIVING GRIEF TIME

Clients raw from loss will often ask me, through their tears, "How long will this take?" Each time I'm asked, I feel a pull of regret that I can't give them a simple answer. Most times I simply have to say, "It takes the time it takes." Diane remembers experts advising that she would return to normal within six months to one year. "There *was* no more normal," says Diane, "so I couldn't understand this 'return to normal.' What could ever be normal after I lost my son? I would never have my old life back. What was normal, back then, could never be again."

I remember one of my favorite spring pastimes growing up in the South was to pull the buds from crepe myrtle trees. Friends and I would take several handfuls of buds and settle down in the shade for a session of "bud bursting." We found that if you squeezed a bud from its base in just the right way, you could make it burst into bloom. The glee was short-lived, though; the petals would soon fall away, leaving the empty husk of the green bud.

Grief is like that bud. Forcing it, trying to muscle through it in order to get more quickly to the other side, only ultimately aborts the process. It simply takes the time it takes. I am reminded of an old Taoist teaching story: Two men on a walk out in nature stopped and admired a waterfall. To their horror, they saw a limp body turning around and around in the tumbling water at the base of the falls, repeatedly appearing and then being sucked back down into the churning water. As they tried to figure out how to retrieve it, they were astonished to see the body finally wash up on the banks of the river, straighten up, shake off the water, and walk toward them, an old man apparently no worse for the wear. In astonishment, they asked, "Old man, how did you not drown? How did you survive?" The old man smiled, bowed to them, and replied, "Simple. You go up when the water goes up. You go down when the water goes down." What is most important is to be able to stay present to your grief as it unfolds, going up as it takes you up, going down as it takes you down. When we are in deep grief, we want a timetable, we want an end to it. We want to regain some sense of control by thinking that this deep grief will be over in exactly three months. We are terrified of drowning in our grief, going down one last time and never coming up for air again.

As I learned through my successive traumas to soften into the grief and trust the process, I discovered that grief was neither a deep sea in which I would drown nor a linear, cookbook process. Some nights I did feel as if I were drowning, but I learned that the feeling, not me, would ultimately dissolve. Like the lazy Susan, each feeling would appear, grow, crest, and subside. I discovered in a very deep way that the Buddhists are right: Everything is impermanent. This means that not only buildings, plants, and even mountains pass away, but feelings pass away through us, too. Some feelings stay on for days or weeks; others move through in hours or even minutes.

Some of you will experience intense emotions like being on a roller coaster (one client called it "emotional whiplash"). For others, the feelings may be quieter but no less deep. Some of us need to shout and wail; others of us need to go deep into nature and sit leaning against a tree for a long time. Some of us move through our grief by talking, some by doing hard gardening or hiking, and some by entering deep into silence.

When you have the time to do your grieving, do it, whether it's by listening to the saddest music you know or by curling up and beating a pillow. When you're heading to an unavoidable meeting at work, make a specific date with yourself to return to the grief: "At seven o'clock tonight I will give myself an hour for this." When seven o'clock comes, honor it in whatever way best fits your process.

Remember also to give yourself conscious breaks when you're feeling lighter: Treat yourself to lunch out, rent a movie, read the funnies. "Grief is like the wind," writes Barbara Ascher in *Landscape without Gravity: A Memoir of Grief*. "When it's blowing hard, you adjust your sails and run before it. If it blows too hard, you stay in the harbor, close the hatches, and don't take calls. When it's gentle, you go sailing, have a picnic, take a swim."

Take your grief one day at a time. When we're in deep grief, we often feel that it will go on forever. Fresh with grief from my divorce, waking up in grief and crying myself to sleep, I was afraid (even though I knew better, in my mind) that I would spend a great deal of the rest of my life waking up sad and going to sleep on a wet pillow. It was easy for me, in that very vulnerable state, to despair of ever feeling better.

I walked around Green Lake with a dear friend on one of those days. She reminded me to take it one day at a time. I told her, on that particular day, that even a day felt overwhelming and endless. She stopped, gave me a big hug, and suggested that on that particular day, I take it one hour at a time, or even one breath at a time. Her suggestion helped me a lot over the following month.

If you find yourself getting trapped in your grief, as I did, afraid of that moment endlessly replicating itself, gently but firmly tell yourself, "Stop," either out loud or silently. Take a deep breath and bring yourself back to the present moment. With as much compassion for yourself as you can find, come back to the present moment and gently remind yourself that grief takes the time it takes.

FINDING AND RECEIVING SUPPORT

We're not meant to do the journey of grief alone.

This is a hard concept for us to understand. We are a nation of Marlboro men and women: Setting our jaw, we ride off into the sunset by ourselves to do our lonely work. I remember being punished and sent to my room as a child, and being told not to come out until I could put a smile on my face. Men were told as boys that only sissies cry.

Diane Nares found support in the community of a small bereavement group of other parents who had lost children. It took her four months to feel ready to attend; she found that getting there for the first time was the biggest challenge. Diane discovered a tremendous common bond with the other grieving parents: "It helped me not feel so alone in a dreadful situation. I had been writing in my journal, but I found that talking out loud about my pain really helped. We ended up really committed to one another; we needed each other and wanted to be there for each other." Diane also found that she needed additional support and began seeing one of the group facilitators for private sessions.

Diane found, as many of us do, that support can come in many forms. Friends were tremendously important in her grieving process, as was her dog, a lab mix she and her husband had brought home for Emilio a year before he died. In addition to group support and therapy, Diane found support in meditation, yoga, and massage, spiritual study, friends, and being out in nature. "Meditation was a real healing force for me. I had practiced meditation before I lost Emilio, but it had new meaning after he died. My mind was in such turmoil, it helped quiet it down and give me a break from everything to turn inward." Diane rediscovered yoga at a retreat six months after Emilio died. "Yoga gave me a means of release, a physical release. It was like physical meditation for me. It evoked feelings, and released so much emotion. It was like massage that first year; both yoga and massage would take me to a place where all my resistance let down and I could cry and cry."

Diane also found solace and support in nature. She loved to go to the ocean and watch the sunset, or walk the canyons where she and Emilio had spent so much time. "Not only would I feel Emilio, but I'd also feel the presence of God. Several times it felt like large arms were around me, holding me and comforting me. It was so powerful at first I couldn't breathe or move; then I just cried and cried. After the pain passed, while out in nature, I'd feel such a wonderful feeling—hope and beauty and a vastness beyond myself—taking me right out of 'me' and into how huge and ultimately okay it all is."

Identify the kind of support that fits your own needs, not what someone else thinks you should do. Think about the methods you've used in the past to deal with grief or severe stress. If you're a talker, find someone or a group, or both, with whom you can talk. If you need to be more internal, try meditation or yoga. Be alert for what works, and what doesn't work—you will know. If the things you've done in the past don't work this time, seek help to find out what will.

Jason, whom you met in Chapter Two, always thought that therapy was for "wimps." Therapy was the furthest thing from his mind until his manager at work, watching his slipping job performance and increasing isolation from coworkers, suggested he give it a try.

"I told her she was even crazier than me," Jason recalled with a grin, at his last session with me after six months of hard work. "Then I figured, why not? Nothing else seemed to be working. I'd tried everything else I knew. I did it out of total desperation, and it was one of the best decisions I've ever made. I learned I could trust someone else to help when I felt awful; it was the first time I'd ever done that. Making the decision to ask for help was 80 percent of the battle. After that, things got easier."

You may surprise yourself, as a loner, opening up to a group for the first time and feeling deeply supported in that way. You may surprise yourself, as an extrovert, by needing to take long walks in nature or by getting off by yourself to write in your journal or listen to sad music. One of my friends, a self-identified "raging extrovert," was surprised to find that what most supported her after the loss of her husband was rocking in her rocking chair, imagining at the same time that she was being held, and rocked, in the loving arms of Mary, mother of Jesus.

Gretchen Schodde created a support team after her diagnosis of lymphoma. Living at a retreat center too far away from support groups, with friends and loved ones scattered all over the country, she created an e-mail team with whom she regularly shared her thoughts, feelings, requests for prayers, and news about her treatment and recovery. "That care team got me through one of the hardest times of my life," Gretchen recalls. "I didn't know how this idea would work via e-mail. What I found, though, was when I requested prayers for healing, or for support for my next round of chemo, I could literally feel the waves of prayers and support wash over me. People responded, too, by e-mail. I kept all those e-mails and read them when I was feeling down." Gretchen discovered that the e-mails she sent were being forwarded by her support team to many others. She ended up being prayed for by hundreds of people around the country. "What started out so awful, the cancer, brought me an amazing gift: the feeling of being prayed for, and cared for, by so many others. It's what got me through."

You can create your own support team, virtual or otherwise. Many have found it helpful to have a "captain" for the team, a close friend or family member who can organize and delegate supportive tasks and errands to be done, put out specific prayer requests, or manage an e-mail group. Your care team can also include professionals who support you, such as therapists, ministers, and massage practitioners.

SELF-COMPASSION

Jennifer Louden, a coach and the author of *The Woman's Comfort Book*, bemoans how we have learned to browbeat ourselves in the name of self-care. "Most of us learn subtle violence towards ourselves as a way of supposed self-care; you know, 'when the going gets tough, the tough get going.' As I began to study the principles of non-violence, I learned that I didn't have to bully myself; I could treat myself lovingly the way I might treat a child or a beloved pet. I now ask my clients, 'How can you practice loving non-violence toward yourself? What could you do in this moment to love yourself?'"

My life changed one afternoon during a therapy session for dealing with the grief of losing a partner. I was criticizing myself for not moving through it sooner, for bursting into tears or becoming irritated at awkward moments, for not handling the loss with more finesse and grace. After I had finished my litany of self-judgment, my therapist simply looked at me for a moment with soft eyes. "What would it be like for you," she gently asked me, "to be compassionate toward yourself as someone in deep pain doing the best she can?"

Be compassionate toward myself? I was struck by the revolutionary quality of her question. It was one I had never considered, and a concept that had never occurred to me. I now see the same startled expression on the faces of clients to whom I put that same question when they are in deep grief.

I returned home that afternoon intrigued by my therapist's suggestion. That evening as I practiced *Metta* meditation (a Buddhist practice of offering goodwill and compassion first toward oneself, then toward others), I realized that I had always passed over the first part—offering Metta toward myself—very quickly, staying in my head rather than my heart. I would drop into my heart only when I offered Metta to others, which I thought of as the "important" part of the meditation. I was shutting myself off from receiving compassion from my own heart each time I practiced Metta.

The realization stunned me. I took a deep, slow breath and watched the leaves on the cherry tree outside the window shimmer in the breeze and the hazy gold light of sunset. *What if I made space for me in my own heart, not only when I was confident and secure, but when I was at the bottom of my own life? How would it be to extend compassion toward myself when I felt most broken and unlovable?*

I realized I would never know until I tried. I closed my eyes, acknowledged my anxiety, breathed into my heart, and said silently to myself:

May I be at peace.
May I be free from suffering.
May I be healed.
May I know the light of my own true nature.

On the first try, I found myself going in and out of awareness; this was very new territory. I took several deep breaths and imagined myself as my small daughter in pain, feeling the love and compassion I felt for her after a skinned knee.

I tried again:

> *May I be at peace.*
> *May I be free from suffering.*
> *May I be healed.*
> *May I know the light of my own true nature.*

It was easier the second time. My heart felt softer and lighter. There was indeed room for me, at my most broken, in my own heart. I did Metta a third time for myself, this time saying it out loud with as much love and compassion as I could let into my heart.

So this is how self-compassion feels. The grief was still there, but I wasn't contracted around it in self-judgment. My grief seemed to float in a larger, softer, and lighter space. I remembered a story about the Buddha being asked what to do with deep pain. He took a handful of salt and dropped it into a tiny cup of water. He then took the same amount of salt and poured it into the lake on whose shores he was standing. With that simple teaching he showed us that we can't control the salt—the pain—that often pours into our lives. What we can do, though, is make the container bigger, to create more space for the same amount of salt, to allow the pain to float in a bigger space, rather than tightly contract. I realized that evening that through extending Metta to myself with a soft heart, I had done just that: made my "container" for the grief more spacious.

Sometimes, there is nothing we can "do" for such deep pain except to make the container bigger. There are many times in therapy when I simply hold loving witness to someone's deep grief. Being in such pain is a profound opportunity, and a new one for many of us, to be able to care for ourselves when we are at our most broken. As we cultivate our ability to do so, we are practicing opening our hearts to ourselves, to life, and to others, in a radically new way.

As I learned to practice this holding my own and others' pain compassionately, without having to "fix" or "rescue," I understood more deeply the ancient Jewish saying: "The only whole heart is a broken heart."

May you learn to swim with your grief, going up when the water goes up, going down when the water goes down. May you receive support from others, and learn the grace of compassionately witnessing your own pain.

May your broken heart become a whole heart.

Interlude Three

GRIEF RITUAL

Ritual is a ceremony done with an intention for healing, celebrating, transforming, mourning, creating, or connecting with the Divine. It is a doorway through which we move from the details of our personal lives into another dimension, time beyond time, healing time, or *kairos*. During ritual, the powers of healing and the sacred are available for us all to call upon. Ritual lifts us out of the strictly personal dimensions of our lives and opens us to the Big Story, the overarching powers of Spirit. Ritual may be as elaborate as a Catholic High Mass or the Japanese Tea Ceremony, or as simple as lighting a candle before a photograph of a loved one who is ill.

Ritual has been used in every culture throughout history to help people move through and heal from grief. These rituals may be part of a religious tradition that enumerates all the steps down to the tiniest detail, or may arise from more individualized or even spontaneous spiritual experiences.

I will be giving you ideas for ritual throughout *Silver Linings*. They're like recipes: Feel free to follow them exactly, or play with them by substituting different ingredients. The most important thing is that the ritual be meaningful for you. If it isn't, it won't work. What follows is a ritual for honoring, grieving, and releasing your losses. Here is a list of things you'll need:

- Small slips of paper
- A pen or pencil
- Black thread or string cut into six-inch lengths
- A Pyrex bowl or other container that can withstand fire
- Matches

- Tissues
- Water for emergency extinguishing
- Approximately 30 minutes of uninterrupted private time

Gather your supplies in a place where you can safely burn paper in a bowl or pot (outside is best; be careful not to set off fire alarms inside). You may perform this ritual by yourself, or have trusted friends, partners, or family for witnesses. Announce, silently or out loud, that your intention for this ritual is to name and help to heal your many losses from trauma. If you wish, pray for whatever spiritual presences you wish to be with you, guiding and supporting you. Get quiet and begin to write down, one per slip of paper, your losses. Remember to include the intangibles, the "dis-es," of your trauma. If you wish, when you've "run out," allow your nondominant hand to write a few more.

When you feel done, read each loss out loud: *I, ___, now release from my life.* You may ring a bell once after each one, to mark the loss. When you have read the slip of paper out loud, roll it up, tie it with a piece of string, and place it in your bowl. Light them with a match, and remember to keep breathing as you watch them burn.

When all are reduced completely to ashes, do one of two things: Either release the ashes in water (outside is best, but under a faucet will do if you have no other options), or, if you have a garden, work them into the dirt (roses and lilacs love ashes). Whatever you do, say a brief prayer that your grief may ultimately turn into new life, so that the ashes of your loss will feed the plants and bring forth new blossoms.

METTA MEDITATION FOR ONESELF

Metta, or Loving-kindness, is a powerful form of Buddhist meditation for opening the heart. The traditional form always starts with Metta to oneself because if our hearts are closed to our own lives, our own joys and pains, it will be difficult, if not impossible, to open our hearts to others. From there, one extends Metta to a loved one, to someone neutral (an acquaintance, a neighbor, a coworker), then to someone who's challenging to care about, and, finally, to all sentient beings.

We will start simply with giving Metta to ourselves. The whole notion of extending love, care, and compassion to ourselves when we are suffering is new for most of us. You will have an opportunity to learn the rest of Metta meditation later in your journey, and later on in the book. For right now, give your own shattered self the immense gift of your own heart.

You may include Metta as part of a more formal meditation. You can also practice offering it to yourself while taking a walk, washing the dishes, or riding the bus. It's about practicing opening your heart to yourself and learning to live in a way that is self-compassionate.

When you are ready, take a deep breath in and release it, emptying yourself. If you wish, you may touch your heart lightly to bring your awareness there. Then repeat to yourself, out loud or silently:

May I be at peace.
May I be free from suffering.
May I be healed.
May I know the light of my own true nature.

Take another deep breath, release, and do a quick body scan. I notice I often tighten up when extending Metta to myself, resisting my own loving-kindness. Soften, take another breath, and offer Metta to yourself again:

May I be at peace.
May I be free from suffering.
May I be healed.
May I know the light of my own true nature.

Continue this for as long as you like. It is very powerful to give yourself ten minutes or so of Metta as a gift. I find it to be equally powerful to extend to myself when I'm waiting at a stoplight, or when I find myself muttering under my breath to other drivers in traffic jams. Give this compassion to yourself as the last thing before you go to sleep; allow it to be a gift that you offer yourself upon awakening. During my own times of initiation, when I would wake up at

2:00 A.M. feeling anxious, heavy-hearted, or overwhelmed, I'd lie in the darkness with one hand on my heart and the other hand on my belly, touching myself gently as I might a frightened child, and repeating Metta for myself. It is a powerful way to call your spirit back wherever you are, no matter what the circumstances.

If this particular set of words doesn't speak to you, experiment with what you'd like to offer yourself. There are hundreds of different wordings for Metta. There is no one magic formula. What would you most like to offer yourself? What would you most like to receive? Make it no longer than four or so offerings, for the sake of memorizing it. When you've found something that works, stick with it, and simply allow yourself to receive it more deeply into your heart and soul each time you repeat it.

4
Entering into the Mystery

"Unless a grain of wheat falls into the earth and dies, it remains alone; but if it dies, it bears much fruit."

I remember reading Jesus's words in college, before I had experienced my first trauma, and thinking, "Hmm, yeah, that's right." It sounded interesting and profound, but irrelevant.

His words touch me deeply thirty years later. They now make sense. Not cognitive sense: My mind doesn't like this idea of dying (literal or metaphorical) now any more than it did thirty years ago. The mind would do anything to avoid literal or even metaphorical death. It would rather carry on a limited, circumscribed life free of suffering than suffer the uncertainties and pain of a death/rebirth experience, even if that experience ultimately gave rise to a deeply renewed life.

But it does make sense to my heart and soul. After the traumas of recovered sexual abuse memories, life-threatening illness, divorce, and loss of a vocational dream, my life is—against all reason—far richer than I ever dreamed possible.

I had dinner with a recovering alcoholic who has spent the last thirty years helping others recover from addiction.

You know, Larona told me, *I used to think of my alcoholism as a curse, which I then somehow moved beyond to get to the blessing of my post-addiction life. I told people that I worked with, "Your curse will turn into your blessing."*

But then something amazing occurred to me about ten years ago, when I was working with an ex-addict who was turning her life around in amazing ways. As we were talking, this quiet voice inside me said, "Larona, your curse is your blessing."

Whoa! That voice stopped me in my tracks. I had to think about it for a long time because I was so used to seeing my alcoholism as a curse, and only a curse. And you know what I discovered? That voice was right. It didn't make sense, but it was right. My life would not be so good and full today if I hadn't been through the hell I'd been through and learned what I learned as a result. If anyone had tried to tell me that alcoholism was a blessing in the early stages of my recovery, I would have told them to beat it. But now, looking back, it's so true. If an angel came down and asked me if I wanted to trade in my experience for something less awful, I would now say, "No way." I am who I am now—full of gratitude for life, listening to God every step of the way—because of all that awfulness. I wouldn't trade it for the world, and now I'm grateful to it as a blessing, not just as a curse. It's a total mystery to me.

MYSTERY

How can a curse be a blessing? How does dying give birth to new life? How could something as blighted as a life-threatening illness, the death of a parent or partner or child, a heart-wrenching divorce, yield blossom and fruit? How can we open to the meaning in circumstances that we didn't want to experience?

Centuries before Jesus, men and women in ancient Greece reenacted yearly the drama of the goddess Demeter and her daughter Persephone, who was raped and abducted to the Underworld. Demeter's sorrow and devastation brought winter to the earth as she searched for her daughter, and the recovery of her daughter from the Underworld brought spring, and new life, back to the earth. In these Eleusinian Mysteries, initiates underwent difficult ordeals in order to learn about the power of death and rebirth, and the mysteries that animate all life.

Descent into the Mysteries allows the initiate to be permanently altered "by the willingness to enter and be worked upon by the elemental forces that live in the domain of the unknown and unknowable," writes Deena Metzger, who has gone to Greece many times to enact a contemporary version of the rites. "This is not descending into chaos, though it feels chaotic when we are there. It is entering into domains that cannot be understood in the ways we generally seek and convey understanding."

Ancient initiates were called *mystes*, derived from the ancient Greek word *myein*, meaning "to close (eyes or mouth)." The traditional interpretation of *mystes* is that the initiates were not to disclose to others what they saw and heard during the rites. I believe there is a deeper meaning. During their initiation, in the darkness, their physical eyes were rendered useless so they could see truth with their inner spiritual eyes; in the silence, mouths closed, they understood those truths, which could never be adequately articulated verbally.

From the work *myein* also comes Mystery, *mysterion*, which originally meant "divine secret." Those early *mystes* heard this divine secret that echoes but prefigures Jesus's wisdom:

> *Unless a grain fall into the ground and die*
> *It cannot grow into an ear of corn.*
> *With your death, you are awakened.*
> *This is the mystery of Eleusis.*

Mystery. Your Mystery, your trauma. It is not a Mystery in the manner of a detective novel—a knot of clues to be cognitively untangled for the final answer—but rather a Mystery to stand in awe of, while barefoot on holy ground (like Moses before the burning bush, amazed that something alive may burn, yet not be consumed). Mystery cannot be controlled or figured out with the rational mind; it must be "lived into" and apprehended with the heart, the soul, the inner spiritual eyes and ears. John Keats, a Romantic poet, called this capacity to live into Mystery a "negative capability," or an ability to exist "in uncertainties, mysteries, and doubts, without any irritable reaching after fact or reason."

Authentic engagement with Mystery—as is happening with you, as a *mystes*—is utterly transforming. Standing barefoot on the holy ground of our unfathomable trauma, immolated in the fires of grief and pain, we die to our old life, never to return to that world.

Philip Simmons, a modern mystic (*mystes!*) consciously traversing his own suffering, crippled and dying from Lou Gehrig's disease, writes in *Learning to Fall: The Blessings of an Imperfect Life:*

> At one time or another, each of us confronts an experience so powerful, bewildering . . . or terrifying that all our efforts to see it as a "problem" are futile. Each of us is brought to the cliff's edge. At such moments we can either back away in bitterness or confusion, or leap forward into mystery. And what does mystery ask of us? Only that we be in its presence, that we fully, consciously, hand ourselves over. That is all, and that is everything.

I remember Dolores, a participant at one of Harmony Hill's cancer retreats, shaking her head in utter amazement at her experience of ovarian cancer:

> I just don't understand. My heart keeps telling me that this cancer is a gift, even though the rest of me hates it, really hates it. I've received this extraordinary gift. I wouldn't trade what I've discovered about myself, or how I've reengaged with God, for anything. I feel more alive—I am more alive—than I've ever been, or dreamed of being. The only catch is that the wrapping sucks. The gift comes in the worst wrapping I could ever think of—cancer. I can't get to the gift unless I'm willing to deal with the wrapping. It doesn't make sense, but it's true.

Opening to the Mystery of your trauma is very different from searching for a reason "why" it happened, the purpose behind it, or a solution. Compulsively looking for reasons aborts the transformational process. Stepping into the Mystery gives trauma meaning and a healing, transformational context. The "reason" that tragedy strikes is not for initiation, any more than the "reason" that lightning strikes is for the "purpose" of a forest fire. The "gift" of tragedy can be initiation, a radical opening of the heart, just as the "gift" of a lightning strike can be a renewed ecosystem; many seeds can open only in the terrific holocaust of a forest fire, just as many spiritual gifts can "open" only from a direct experience of trauma, death, and rebirth. A client once brought me this poem by Rashani, which I now have workshop participants read as we honor Mystery:

> *There is a brokenness out of which comes the unbroken,*
> *a shatteredness out of which blooms the unshatterable.*
>
> *There is a sorrow beyond all grief which leads to joy*
> *and a fragility out of whose depths emerges strength.*
>
> *There is a hollow space too vast for words through which*
> *we pass with each loss,*
> *out of whose darkness we are sanctioned into being.*
>
> *There is a cry deeper than all sound whose serrated edges cut the heart*
> *as we break open*
> *to the place inside which is unbreakable and whole, while learning to sing.*

CONSCIOUS PARTICIPATION

So why I am telling you this about Mystery and initiation? Why don't I just stick with the physical and psychological "facts" of trauma?

Because acknowledging and honoring yourself as a mystes, a journeyer into the Mysteries, and as an initiate undergoing the trials of life-bestowing initiation can make a significant difference both in the quality of your healing journey and in its outcome.

Conscious participation in the Mysteries confers depth and meaning to life. "As long as you do not practice it, this dying and becoming," writes poet Rainer Maria Rilke, "you are only a dreary guest on the dark earth." When we are struggling in trauma's wake, a map of trauma as a transformational journey can make the difference between a post-trauma life that is larger and more authentic and a life that is smaller and embittered.

Naming yourself as an initiate, as a *mystes*, honors who you are. It counters how you may feel at this point—broken, grieving, angry, helpless—with the larger picture that this very brokenness is part of a powerful sacred journey, "a shatteredness out of which blooms the unshatterable."

This larger picture recently made a big difference in my life. One September morning in 2001, I was awakened from deep sleep by a panicked coworker at Harmony Hill, who told me that our country was under attack. Like hundreds of thousands of other Americans on Tuesday, September 11, I ricocheted between dazed shock and tears of grief and terror as I watched the towers crumble, over and over, on the news. I realized several days later, while walking in a Seattle park for solace, *I am in initiation. We, as a country, are in collective initiation. We have utterly lost the old assurances and beliefs about safety and control. I feel—we all feel—terribly vulnerable in a world gone mad.*

After working with trauma and initiation for twenty years, I recognized the hallmarks of an initiatory journey. This recognition didn't erase my feelings of fear, terrible grief, or radical uncertainty about the future. But it did give me a map of the process I would have to go through, with all its challenges and gifts: a call to action to care for myself as a vulnerable initiate, and a certainty that, if I walked clear-eyed into the Mystery, I would emerge on the other side with new gifts and graces and a deeper faith in the abiding presence of the Divine.

I spent much of the year after 9/11 working with groups and individuals around collective initiation, assisting them to work consciously with the process. It has given hope to many and allowed them to surrender heart and soul more deeply into the amazing process and unfolding of which we are all a part. Conscious participation has empowered them to take compassionate action, care more deeply for others as well as for themselves, open to a profound level of spiritual trust, and ultimately break open into a spiritual joy that is independent of outer circumstances. What better gifts than these?

Thinking of herself as an initiate transformed how Andrea dealt with the emotional and spiritual aftermath of the terrorist attack. Before attending my workshop "9/11 as an Initiation," Andrea says, "I was in kind of a depressed, shocked fog every day. I had a hard time just getting out of bed. There wasn't much that gave me any hope. When I started thinking about myself as an initiate, it gave me power to think in a new way about the whole experience. Maybe there was something here that could break me open, instead of just breaking me down. Maybe I could honor myself and all my feelings, and put them in a larger context. Maybe there could be new life at the end of this, instead of just forever being a diminished version, physically and emotionally, of my former self. As an initiate, I could walk a little taller and be more open to where this journey was leading me and what life was teaching me in the process."

CROSSING THE THRESHOLD

Most of us settle for the routines and complacencies of everyday life until trauma yanks us out of our comfort zone. In the words of mythologist Joseph Campbell, who articulated the path of the Hero's Journey in all great myths and spiritual stories, trauma is The Call to Adventure. Life raps sharply at our door, just as the wizard Gandalf did at the hobbit-hut of Bilbo Baggins. We are asked to step foot into the unknown territory of initiation, the Hero or Heroine's Journey. Like Bilbo the Hobbit, we may try to refuse the call. Even if our life lies in pieces around us, we may vainly try to piece together that which can never be repaired, like Humpty Dumpty, rather than step across the threshold and begin the journey.

What we learn from the Hero's or Heroine's Journey is that, once the call to initiation, to adventure, is issued, we can never go back, no matter how hard we try. "Whether small or great, and no matter what the stage or grade of life, the call rings up the curtain, always, on a mystery of transfiguration, a spiritual passage which, when complete, amounts to a dying and a birth," writes Campbell, in *The Hero with a Thousand Faces*. "The familiar horizon has been outgrown; the old concepts, ideals, and emotional patterns no longer fit; the time for a passing of a threshold is at hand."

This passing of the threshold, this step from letting go of the familiar that has now passed, into the second stage of initiation, Wilderness, must be a *conscious* step. We may refuse the Call and spend the rest of our lives attempting to numb the pain through busyness or addiction, or we may take a deep breath and say Yes.

The model of the Hero's and Heroine's Journey shows us that when we say Yes to the journey, the initiation, then grace happens. Allies show up for support and guidance. We start to honor and respect ourselves in new ways. We may not trust, on our own, that rebirth will follow all the trials of our trauma, but we know there is no turning back.

In the Hero's or Heroine's Journey, allies begin to appear as soon as the call is answered and the initiate approaches the threshold into the Wilderness. Allies can take many shapes and forms: small birds who fly ahead to show the path through dense forest, wizards who offer encouragement and wisdom, great bears who carry the heroine or hero over great distances, or angelic beings who offer healing and hope.

Allies can be just as varied in our own "real" journeys. Throughout my long, exhausting sojourn with chronic fatigue syndrome, my cat, Roo, was often my greatest ally. When I was too weak to get up from the couch, Roo stayed with me, her green eyes watching over me. She taught me patience, and the power of simply being in the present moment. I, who had spent a lifetime dashing from task to task, learned from Roo the immense virtue of just breathing and watching life unfold through the window.

"People allies" have graced my initiation journeys as well: partners, good friends, family, psychotherapists, spiritual directors. Some of us lean on trusted friends; others of us look to partners or family. We call upon God, the Buddha, Jesus, Muhammad, Kuan Yin, Mary, and other divine beings. Many of us discover spiritual wisdom figures through dreams and guided imagery, and our own deeper, wiser, Self. I encourage you to find and name your allies as you approach this threshold into the next stage of your initiation. Your allies will cross the threshold with you, giving you guidance, strength, and support for your journey.

Cynthia, a client who was healing from rape, was at an all-time low in trusting people. Since the violent assault, she had withdrawn from friends and family, imprisoned in her private hell. I encouraged her to find a nonhuman ally. Cynthia looked at me as if I were a little crazy (I'm used to that "look" when I suggest this to clients), but agreed to consider it. She returned the following week with a small smile, her first in months: "I thought, 'Why not?' I couldn't imagine asking a person for help. I went out in my back yard to sit against a pine tree and think about it. I thought and thought, and was getting really frustrated, when all of a sudden I realized I was leaning right up against my ally! She had been there all along, and I didn't even know it until I was open to the possibility. I realized, 'I really can trust this tree.' I've been sitting up against her for years when I needed time out."

I encouraged Cynthia to spend a little time each day resting into her ally, feeling the strength and quiet support of the pine. The next session, the smile was a little bigger: "I can't believe I'm doing this, but I'm talking to that tree. I have this feeling that the tree is really listening to me. One time I even stood up and kind of bellied up to the trunk, leaning my face against the bark. I almost felt like the tree was holding me. I cried and cried. After that cry, for the first time since the rape, I felt a kind of peace."

Cynthia continued to work with the tree as her ally, allowing the tree to teach her to send her own "roots" deep into the ground. Cynthia reported the feeling of peace growing as she continued to go sit against the tree and talk to it. "I feel like that tree taught me how to trust again," Cynthia recalled several years later. "She gave me strength for the journey, and a kind of gentle unconditional presence that I desperately needed. After I learned to trust her, I felt like I could begin to make my way back to trusting people, too."

SAYING YES

When you are ready—and you will know the time—you can say Yes and cross the threshold into the next stage of your journey, the Wilderness. This does not mean you are finished with the grief; the grief may continue for quite some time, depending upon the depth and severity of your trauma. What it does mean, though, is that the wild roller-coaster ride of grief and anger is no longer center stage, waking and sleeping. You have moments—perhaps sometimes even hours or days—of ease. You may still be emotionally and physically exhausted, but you find that you now have enough energy to rejoin life in small ways, enough psychic energy to think about taking the next step.

When you make the commitment to seeing your trauma as an initiatory journey, you are ready to cross that threshold into new worlds, and New Life.

When I was healing from childhood sexual abuse, I created a way for myself to consciously cross over that threshold. I first made a "passport" from a folded piece of construction paper. I pasted my photo in it, and wrote and drew aspects of my life that I knew I had to release: old beliefs about safety, control, and inviolability; myths about childhood; a shattered trust in life and God. As an inveterate world traveler, I had had the experience of handing over my passport at international borders before being allowed to cross over into new territory. I always received the passport back. This time, though, I had to permanently surrender this passport, because I knew that I could never go back to what was my "normal life" again. I had to do this in order to move into new territories of healing.

I gave myself several uninterrupted hours to assemble my passport, pasting on the cover a photo taken the previous summer, before I had remembered the sexual abuse. I had spent so much time and energy trying to get back to that person. I now realized that whatever was ahead of me, I would never again be the "me" in that photo.

I laid a length of string across the living room floor, dividing it in half. I stood against one wall and contemplated the threshold ahead of me. I knew that once I surrendered my passport and stepped over that line into Wilderness, there would be no going back. I took my time, step by step, saying farewell to the life I had known. I felt tremendous resistance to stepping over the threshold, and tried to breathe through it. When I reached the string, I said goodbye to the me who once was, to all of her hopes and her beliefs and her expectations about life. Then I laid my passport down, took a deep breath, and stepped over the threshold.

I did it! I had fully committed to my own journey, wherever it took me, trusting (at least at that moment!) that wherever it took me would be deeper into healing and New Life.

Nothing changed instantly; no flashy miracles occurred. However, I *knew* that my life had changed. I was more empowered now. I became an active participant in my own life, rather than constantly feeling like a victim. I felt a deepened sense of the presence of the Divine, and knew that my journey mattered somehow in the great scheme of things, that it had meaning, even if at that point I was not able to fully understand it.

When I facilitate retreats and workshops on life transitions and initiation, I often lead participants through this same process and continue to be astonished at its power. After making their passports, participants must traverse a large space before they finally cross over the rope into the next stage of their journey. I tell them that the threshold only opens in one direction—after they have crossed it, there is no going back. I light a candle, lower the lights, and play soft music as I witness women and men approach their own threshold. Some take a long time before making their first step; others run toward the threshold and then stop right at it, suddenly aware of its importance. Others approach thoughtfully, step by step, sit down to weep, or actually retreat for a while to think more about the whole process.

Once over the threshold, some dance, some cry, some look about in wonder. Almost all feel deeply the impact of consciously stepping over that threshold and saying Yes to the rest of their healing journey.

"The journey of 10,000 miles begins with one step," the ancient Chinese sage Lao-Tzu said. When you are ready, step over your threshold and come with me into Wilderness, the place of profound healing and growth.

Interlude Four

To work with this visualization, you have several options:

• Read the visualization into a cassette recorder and play it back for yourself. Whenever you see "(. . .)" be silent for several seconds.
• Have a friend either record the visualization or read it to you.
• Read the script several times and simply recreate it as you visualize.

Know that people "visualize" in many different ways. You may see in fine detail and gorgeous color; you may smell, taste, or feel; or you may simply "know" what is happening without any cues at all. These are all ways of "knowing," and all are valid.

In this meditation, you'll meet a Wisdom Guide, from whom you'll receive wisdom and support. A Wisdom Guide might be a religious figure like Mary, a saint, or Quan Yin, the Buddhist goddess of compassion. It might be a relative, alive or long dead; it might be a favorite pet or an animal you've never had personal contact with, such as a jaguar. Or this Wisdom Guide might be simply that: an older man or woman who seems very loving and wise. The right one for this part of your journey will come to you.

Find a quiet room where you can be undisturbed for about thirty minutes. Have your initiation journal and a pen or pencil with you for recording your journey and any insights you receive afterward. Find a comfortable position, sitting up or lying down (if you're tired, sit up to avoid falling asleep).

Take a deep breath and allow yourself to feel the support of the chair or bed. Sink into this support. (. . .) Allow it to receive your weight. (. . .) Take several more deep breaths, allowing yourself to relax more and more deeply with each breath taken. (. . .) As you breathe, gently move your awareness through your body. If you find any place of holding or tension, gently breathe into and around the tension, allowing it to soften, and release it on the outbreath.

And now, imagine a healing place, a place that feels safe and peaceful. (. . .) It may be a beloved place from childhood, a favorite vacation haunt, an imaginary place from a book or movie. (. . .) When you're "there," look around. (. . .) Allow it to become real, very real. (. . .) What do you see before you? Behind you? What special sounds do you hear? Feel the texture of whatever you're sitting or standing on. (. . .) Feel the sun on your face, or the wind in your hair, or the cool shade on your skin. (. . .) How does it feel in your body and in your heart to be in this safe place? Breathe in the healing qualities of this place. (. . .) Feel your heart opening and softening, so safe. (. . .)

When you are ready, ask to meet a Wisdom Guide who can help you on your healing journey. Invite one into your healing space. (. . .) This Guide may be a religious figure, a deceased relative, an animal ally, a mythical figure such as a wise old man or woman, a being of light. (. . .) Invite them in. (. . .) When you have a sense of the Guide's presence, whether visually, or in your body, or just by knowing, welcome the Guide, in whatever way feels most appropriate. (. . .) If you wish, ask the Guide's name. (. . .) You may find yourself conversing with your Guide, or you may find yourself directly communicating, heart to heart, without spoken words. (. . .)

This Wisdom Guide understands your particular journey and its challenges and gifts. This Guide understands all your feelings, sees you completely. Feel this Guide's compassion for your pain. Look into the Guide's eyes, and receive the Guide's healing love for you. (. . .) You may ask this Wisdom Guide any question about your journey if you wish. (. . .) The Wisdom Guide may answer you in words, in images, a song, a feeling, or simply a "knowing." (. . .) Ask this Guide for guidance and support for whatever is closest to your heart right now. (. . .) And now, simply allow the gaze of this being to fill you with their love and total acceptance of you and your journey. (. . .)

If you wish, you may ask your Wisdom Guide for a healing gift for your journey. Hold your hands out and receive this gift. This gift may be an object, an image or symbol, a word, a song. You may see or feel it in your hands, or simply know it's there.

Receive this now. (. . .) Thank your Wisdom Guide for the gift. Raise your hands and place this gift in your heart. (. . .) Feel the gift sink deep into the safe recesses of your heart. Know that, from this time on, you carry your gift within you and can call it forth whenever you need it. (. . .) Thank your Wisdom Guide in whatever way you'd like for this gift, and for the guidance. (. . .) Know that you can call upon your Guide whenever you need wisdom. (. . .) Bring yourself back to your breath. (. . .) Slowly and gently return to the room, bringing back all you have received. (. . .)

Stretch and reorient yourself to your physical surroundings, coming back into the awareness of your physical body.

Record your journey in the first section of your journal. If you wish, you can draw the gift your Wisdom Guide gave you and write about ways you might "use" this gift in your journey. Please know that when I suggest you draw anything, I am not talking about creating art. Simple sketches are just as powerful and healing as beautiful or technically correct ones. The power of drawing anything is that it amplifies an energy already present in your heart and soul. Let go of any notions of how it "should" look because it is just for you.

You may place the drawing or other symbolic representation of your healing gift on your altar. Light a candle and ask that it continue the healing work in your heart. If you can find a photo, icon, artwork, or small statue of your Wisdom Guide, you can put it on your altar too.

PART TWO:
WILDERNESS

5
Journeying through Wilderness

Going into the Wilderness is part of our ancient spiritual heritage: Jesus in the wilderness. Innana's sojourn in the Underworld. Buddha's itinerant search for enlightenment. The Israelites, their bonds of slavery broken, wandering in the wilderness on their way to the Promised Land. Mohammed on his desert journey. Isis wandering throughout the Egyptian world after the death of her husband. Arthur's knights wandering in the forest for five years in search of the Holy Grail.

Physical terrain is a powerful metaphor for the inner landscape—the state of mind and spirit—of heroes and heroines in the great myths and spiritual stories. These heroines and heroes make a journey into new and unknown territory, and they are utterly changed in the process. They come to terms with their destiny in the Wilderness, receive guidance about their next stage in life, are tested, and are ultimately transformed. Time spent alone in the Wilderness allows them to shed attachments to everyday life, and their former self, effecting deep transformation by discovering what is most real, most vital, and most enduring.

"The literature of mysticism and mythology the world over speaks of transformation as a journey to another land," writes transpersonal psychologist Ralph Metzner in *The Unfolding Self*. "The experience of change and the experience of wandering are very similar. In German, 'to change' is *wandeln*; 'to wander' is *wandern*. As we wander we change. The pilgrim who arrives at the sacred place is not the same person who left home. The seeker who returns to her family or tribe, bringing gifts of power, healing, or vision, is a transformed individual."

All of us settle into the familiar comfort of what society considers normal or "reality." We blindly and unquestioningly follow cultural beliefs and mores, metaphorically asleep at the wheel of our own lives. How many of us remember what the sky looked like as we commuted to work this morning, or even remember the commute itself? What is the texture of the skin on your lover's neck? Your baby's hand? How long has it been since you and another gazed at each other and really saw the Light of the Beloved shining through? Most spiritual traditions assert that we are "asleep" for much, if not most, of our lives, completely ensnared in mundane reality. The purpose of the spiritual journey, say these same traditions, is to "wake up." Being awake (the word "Buddha" actually means "One who is awake") is our birthright. We are born with this connection to the Divine but become disconnected as we are assimilated into the frenzied unconsciousness of our culture.

"Waking up" is what happens in Wilderness. In this stage, we open our eyes from the sleep of mass consciousness. Everything is different. As a sojourner in your own Wilderness, you have left behind the known, the comfortable, and the familiar. Sometimes we need to become "lost" in order to find who we really are, what really animates and drives our lives at the deepest level. Poet David Wagoner rephrases a Native American's instructions to a vision quester in his poem "Lost":

> Stand still. The trees ahead and the bushes beside you
> Are not lost. Wherever you are is called Here,
> And you must treat it as a powerful stranger,
> Must ask permission to know it and be known.

WILDERNESS

Imagine for a moment being in literal wilderness, hundreds of miles from anything known. You have left behind your "normal" life. Cars are useless, as there are no highways, no roads. It's hard sometimes to know which way to go: In the wilderness, there aren't even any paths.

It's just you, the Wilderness, and Spirit. Your designer suit means nothing out here; neither does your bank account, the make of your car, the prestige of your job (or lack of it), your family pedigree. Gone is the frenetic bustle of computers, cell phones, faxes, and rush-hour traffic. The diversions that disconnect you from your soul—movies, TV, the everyday dramas of our lives—are inaccessible. Your old "identity" simply doesn't matter.

What does matter? Your courage. Your ability to go inside of yourself for guidance and strength. Your receptivity to the presence of the Divine. Your willingness to see who you really are, stripped of all that is impermanent, no matter how tightly you hold on to it. What matters is your willingness to find spiritual bedrock, the ground of your being.

I once took a huge leap (for me) and left Seattle to hike solo for a week in the Cascade wilderness. I was in the throes of a midlife crisis; all that I had worked so hard for felt meaningless. I no longer had any idea "who" I was, where I was going, or what I really wanted. I just needed to be in a place, for a time, where all of that simply didn't matter. I wanted to drive away from all my roles in my life, my calendar, and my cell phone.

As I drove up to Snoqualmie Pass, I felt the weight of all I had been carrying drop from my chest and shoulders. Setting up camp, I found I could really breathe again for the first time in months.

I was scared, particularly when hiking. I knew bears and cougars roamed the area; I knew I could be seriously hurt and might not be rescued for days. What I found, though, was a wild and immense freedom. I could let go of trying so hard to "be" someone when I no longer had any idea of who I was. I thought about Ram Dass's assertion that we are in "Somebody Training" from the moment we are born, trying so hard to be "Someone" in order to impress, get ahead, be loved, or belong. I realized, as I hiked to waterfalls or rested on outcroppings that overlooked range after range of mountains, that I, as a

"Somebody Trainee," had developed a deep fear that who I really was, was not enough.

This fear engendered by "Somebody Training" becomes, for all of us, a low background hum, imperceptible against the noise of contemporary life. However, during trauma or times of great change, that hum can rise to a roar. Trauma issues us an invitation to deeper integrity, offers a rare opportunity to shed that which is no longer us, or never has been: beliefs, identities, neuroses, compulsions to be other than who we truly are.

Wilderness—literal wilderness—became a mirror for me, as it has for so many seekers throughout history, for an interior landscape free of the shackles with which we bind ourselves. Sojourning in the wilderness for that week in the immense silence of the sacred, I honored my lostness as a powerful stranger and recovered some of my Original Self. I called back my spirit from all those behaviors and identities that no longer worked for me. I had the space and time to listen to my own heart beat, to pray for and receive guidance about my life direction, free from the distractions of my everyday life, to be held in the loving arms of Spirit.

"Nature is a proper setting for a return to ourselves, our source, our place of origin," writes Gregg Levoy in *Callings*. "By 'going back to nature' we are, in a sense, returning to the garden, to the place where we were contained within nature's wholeness. We were not separate from the divine, from whence our visions and calls emanate, but in right relationship to the larger forces, as well as our own senses."

I don't know if I'll ever spend a solo week in wilderness again. That week, though, became a touchstone for me of what the stage of Wilderness is truly about: the excitement and terror of going into unknown territory, free of prior restraints of thought and habit, and receiving the great gifts of that freedom.

THE THRESHOLD

If you were an initiate in a tribal culture, you would be sent out in this stage into the literal wilderness. Your exterior landscape would mirror the inner landscape of your heart and soul. You might be sent out for a three-day vision quest as a Native American, a year-long walkabout as an Australian aborigine, or a "year-walk" among the Basques. In tribal cultures, this middle stage, Wilderness, is considered the most powerful and sacred of the three stages of a rite of passage. It is a time when initiates, stripped of their old identity, their old beliefs and certainties, are most open to the numinous and alchemical power of the Divine.

Anthropologists call this middle stage the Liminal stage. Liminal comes from the Greek *limen*, "threshold;" it is the same word found in "subliminal," meaning below the threshold (of awareness). In some ways you crossed a threshold to get here. In a larger sense, though, during this stage you become a threshold dweller. Think of thresholds as doorways from room to room. When you step into a threshold, you are in neither this room or that; you have stepped away from one room and have not yet stepped into another.

Just so with liminality. You have left behind one way of being, replete with its life structure, beliefs, expectations, hopes, and dreams. You have not yet stepped into the next life structure, or way of being (and of course, at this point, it may feel as if you never will). You are neither this nor that—dead to your old life, but not yet born into your new one.

When undergoing major transitions, we seem to be hard-wired to experience this in-between time, an interlude between major life chapters. This interlude seems to serve four major purposes: to set one apart so that one may reflect on one's life and life purpose; to open one wide to the transformative power of the numinous; to create an inner emptiness, a womb that gestates a new sense of self and a new life; and to lead one to trust more deeply in the processes of life, death, and rebirth. Wilderness is an immensely powerful time beyond time, a period of reexamining one's life from the ground up, of resting in the arms of the Divine, and ultimately reconfiguring a renewed life that is in alignment with one's deepest being and purpose. This stage is called by many names, and I'll share some of them with you because the experience of Wilderness is larger than any one descriptor. Each of these descriptors carries a piece of the rich and fertile meaning of this in-between time:

• William Bridges, author of *Transitions*, calls this stage the "neutral zone": "In keeping with our (culture's) mechanistic bias, we have tried to make do with recharging and repair, imagining that renewal comes through fixing something defective or supplying something that is missing. In fact it is only by returning for a time to the formlessness . . . that renewal can take place. The neutral zone is the only source of the self-renewal that we all seek." Bridges has also referred to it as "a place without a name—an empty space in the world and the lifetime within which a new sense of self could gestate."

• Joseph Campbell calls it "The Road of Trials": that part of the initiatory journey where the hero or heroine is tested, is supported by supernatural allies, and discovers his or her own strengths and gifts.

• Tibetan Buddhists call the time between time a *bardo* state. Bardo literally means "suspended between" and signifies a gap or opening. Bardo states represent a profound opportunity to release delusion and embrace clear seeing.

• Jeanne Achterberg, author of *Lightning at the Gate*, calls it "Discovery." Her own experience of cancer and traumatic divorce, as well as a lifetime of working with others in trauma and crisis, led her to conceptualize liminality in this way. "In Discovery, you reconnoiter and think in new and different ways," she told me. "In my own life, it's as if a lightning bolt struck me and said, 'Whoa, girl! Time to do your life very differently.'"

• Jean Shinoda Bolen calls it "forest" in *Crossing to Avalon*: "When we enter a forest phase of our lives, we enter a period of wandering and a time of potential soul growth. In the forest it is possible to reconnect with our own innate nature, to meet what we have kept in the shadows and what we have been kept from knowing or acknowledging about ourselves. . . . Here it is possible to find what we have been cut off from, to 're-member' a once vital aspect of ourselves. We may uncover a wellspring of creativity that has been hidden for decades. . . . Most of all, once in the forest, we must find within ourselves what we need to survive."

All of these names describe something essential about this stage, but it is ultimately larger and deeper than any one descriptor. None of these names alone can sufficiently describe the transformational experience. After your sojourn in this place that is not a place, you may come up with your own word or words.

Taking the Time It Takes

What is most important for you to know is that *this stage, by whatever name it is called, has been virtually eliminated by our "modern" culture*. We are advised to get over it, get on with our life, return to "normal." I am reminded of my daughter's favorite computer game when she was younger, called "Frog Crossing." An unfortunate frog had to cross a busy highway to reach its lily-pond home. The point of the game, given the speeding semi-trucks on the road, was to cross as speedily as possible to avoid becoming roadkill. It's as if the rules are posted in bold: DANGER AHEAD! NO REFLECTION TIME ALLOWED! NO SITTING DOWN IN MIDDLE OF HIGHWAY TO PONDER IF THIS IS THE BEST WAY TO CROSS! JUST DO IT!

Our culture sees the Wilderness stage like that highway: dangerous. We are urged to cross to the other side and begin a new life as quickly as possible. The surest way to kill a get-acquainted party conversation is to respond to the opening, "Tell me about yourself," with "At this point in my life, I'm not exactly sure." The eyes of your formerly engaged listener will glaze over, and he or she will quickly make an excuse about having to go get a refill.

Friends, family, and coworkers can sometimes respond the same way. Some may be a source of wonderful support, letting you know they're there for the duration. Others, because of their own anxiety in the face of such unknowns, may urge you to "get on" with your life. They themselves may have turned deaf ears to the Call and refused to cross the threshold, preferring to stay stuck in old patterns rather than risk the journey into new life. "Liminal *personae* nearly always and everywhere are regarded as polluting to those who have never been . . . initiated," writes Victor Turner, one of the earliest anthropologists to describe this process.

We are a nation of the uninitiated, claims poet Robert Bly in *The Sibling Society*. Initiations in tribal cultures brought participants into authentic adulthood and increasing wisdom with each initiation. We instead go for the quick fix: the weekend intensive, medication, and self-help books that promise to painlessly transform our lives in 21 days. As the uninitiated, we lack the skills and the courage to support someone crossing an unknown and utterly mysterious sea.

Here is what I tell my clients and students who sail this unknown sea: *You are Liminal, poised between the Old Story of your life and the New Story. You are an initiate on holy ground. If you were tribal, you would be set apart and honored for your courage and your emptiness. You would be supported and guided by elders, who had undergone the same death and rebirth experience and knew well its terrors, its challenges, and its tremendous gifts.*

"When we set our sights on a higher meaning, we automatically cast ourselves in the role of a dweller at the threshold, an initiate in a Great Story," writes Joan Borysenko in *Fire in the Soul*. "We are passing through the fire on the way to a purification of sufficient value that our suffering becomes worthwhile when weighed against it. Part of the value of suffering and dwelling at the threshold is that it initiates or intensifies the search for what is most sacred, for only in placing our minds on the promise of that sacredness can we emerge from the liminal period not only intact but healed."

You are not part of a tribal culture, but you can honor this time outside of time even if your culture doesn't. You can allow yourself to be in this stage as long as it takes. You can find mentors and "elders" to support and guide you in your journey. If you allow yourself this time, you will make it to another shore, a land perhaps only dreamed of before, a territory of new wholeness, integrity, joy, and life in Spirit. In retrospect, you may look upon this Wilderness time as one of the most important of your entire life. I certainly do. I honor you for being here.

Exploring Wilderness

I often invite participants in life transition retreats to imaginally explore their personal Wilderness. I lead them through the visualization found at the end of this chapter where they discover their own inner landscape. They then collage, paint, draw, or sculpt their own Wilderness. Participants are often astonished at the vividness and dead-on metaphorical accuracy of their visualizations.

Samuel, a self-assured, successful businessman, was brought to his knees by business and personal bankruptcy. He cut a small dead branch into sections and placed them in clay as stumps. "My life used to be green—lots of money, lots of security. Everyone wanted to be my friend. 'Easy Street,' and I loved it. I used to live in a lush green forest with everything growing easy. Now I'm stumbling through a forest of stumps. My life is a clearcut. Nothing's alive."

Deirdre, who had lost her house and all possessions in a fire, put sand in a box top. "That's it. Sand. It's like an endless stretch of desert. I always thought that story about the Israelites wandering through the desert was kind of hokey. I guess I'm out there with them now, and that desert looks awful big."

Anderson, an artist whose husband died suddenly of a heart attack, astonished herself with a very different response. She splashed intense colors across a large poster board. She smiled as she explained that her Wilderness, although very challenging at times, was filled with a vivid intensity of life she had never known before. "I've always worked in pencil, doing very precise portraits and landscapes—everything totally under control. After my husband, Moen, died, I was so heartbroken. I was, and still am, so confused! I have no idea how to not be a wife, but painting like this made me realize I'm now out of some kind of box. Life now has a vividness it's never had before, even if sometimes it's vividly excruciating!"

Lisa, whose vocation as a gym teacher was cut short by multiple sclerosis, created a forest from clay and cedar fronds. She said to Samuel, "I know that your life before felt like a lush green forest, and that felt good for you. Well, living in Utah, I'm used to landscapes where you can see far ahead. Right now, though, I'm in a thick forest without any paths. Just lots and lots and lots of trees. I have no idea where I'm going; I really am wandering. I remember Dante writing about losing his way in a thick wood in the middle of his life. Well, that's me too."

The next five chapters will be your guide to Wilderness. Please know, though, that they are not in a linear order. There is very little linearity in Wilderness! It is indeed a place that is not a place, and a time that is not a time. All of the subject matter of Part Two will happen in its own time, at its own pace. Feel free to read the chapters in the order presented, or skip to the chapter that speaks most to you right now. There is no one "right" way to do Wilderness: Trust the wisdom of your own feet.

Wilderness will be your "home" for the next while, as it has been for so many initiates, heroes, and heroines throughout time and myth. Your sojourn may last weeks. It may last months or even years.

You need not sojourn there alone. Although there are no maps for your particular "Wilderness," other sojourners throughout time have left maps of the process. Their wisdom will be shared with you in the following chapters. Wilderness will challenge you, grace you, and ultimately heal you.

The Israelites wandered in their desert for forty years before finding the Promised Land. Although it was a challenging time, they received manna, bread from heaven, every morning to sustain them for the day's travels. Manna represents the blessings and grace that come to you in Wilderness to nourish your soul. Hosea, a Hebrew prophet, spoke as God talking to the Israelites when he proclaimed, "That is why I am going to lead her (Israel) out into the wilderness and speak to her heart. I am going to give her back her vineyards, and make the valley of Achor ("misfortune" in Hebrew) a gateway of hope."

In Wilderness you will break open to the bedrock of your essential self, free from the fetters of your own "Somebody Training." You will emerge from your time in Wilderness with a new sense of purpose and a deepened connection with yourself, with Spirit, and with others. Wilderness will, in the end, gift you with manna, your own "wild and precious life."

Interlude Five

GUIDED MEDITATION: WILDERNESS

The purpose of this guided meditation is threefold: to discover the landscape of your own inner Wilderness, to receive guidance from your Wisdom Guide about this part of your journey, and to receive a Seeking Name.

Seeking Names, or initiation names, are an important part of many initiations. These are private soul names that recognize the essence of who you are, and who you are becoming. They may be descriptors of qualities, like "Trusting Heart." They may also be elements of the physical world that reflect important qualities, such as "Stream-meets-sea" or "Madrona Wind." They might also come as words or sounds that have no direct correlation to known language, but resonate in the heart or raise goosebumps on the arms.

Close your eyes and let your weight be supported by whatever you are sitting or lying on. Take a deep breath and allow yourself to feel the support of the chair or bed. Sink into this support. (. . .) Allow the chair to receive your weight. (. . .) Take several more deep breaths, allowing yourself to relax more and more deeply with each breath. (. . .) As you breathe, gently move your awareness through your body. If you find any place of holding or tension, gently breathe into and around the tension, allowing it to soften, and release it on the outbreath. (. . .)

Allow yourself now to travel to your own Wilderness. This Wilderness may be some place you've actually visited; it may be a place you've read about or seen in a movie; it may be someplace entirely new. (. . .)

Explore this place now. What does it look like before you? Turn around and see what is behind you. (. . .) What is the ground like beneath your feet? What sounds do you hear? Notice how it feels to be in your own Wilderness. (. . .) Take some time to explore this new place. (. . .) What does the landscape of this place tell you about your own journey into inner Wilderness?

(. . .)

Invite your Wisdom Guide to be with you now. (. . .) Welcome them into your Wilderness, and allow the Guide to respond. (. . .) Your dialogue may take place through words, images, feelings, or simply speaking heart to heart. (. . .)

What would you most like guidance and support for now? Drop into your heart and discover. (. . .) Share this with your Wisdom Guide, and receive the Guide's response. (. . .) Ask the Guide anything for which you would like guidance now. (. . .)

And, when you are ready, ask your Guide now for your Seeking Name to honor yourself as an initiate. If nothing comes, play with making one up from what first comes to you, even if it doesn't make sense. (. . .) When you receive it, say it to yourself. (. . .) Let it roll off your tongue, over and over. (. . .) This name should make you feel good, feel strong, feel honored. (. . .) Breathe your Seeking Name into your heart, where you may carry it wherever you go. (. . .) If you wish, you may dance your name in your Wilderness, sing your name, or simply be with it, with your Guide. (. . .) Ask your Guide to tell you about your Seeking Name, and how to best use it in your journey. (. . .)

And now, thank your Wisdom Guide for guidance and for your Seeking Name. (. . .) Know that you can continue to draw upon your Guide's wisdom and help whenever you need it. Take one more look around your Wilderness, knowing that this is holy ground. (. . .)

Allow yourself to slowly and gently return to the room and present time, bringing back with you your Seeking Name, and all that you have learned and experienced. (. . .)

Stretch and reorient yourself to your physical surroundings, coming back into the awareness of your physical body.

Your seeking name will be your own private soul-name, a powerful gift to you from Spirit. Say it to yourself to call your own spirit back when you are frightened, anxious, or needing strengthening and grounding. Sing or chant it to yourself. When you take a walk, listen to the wind calling you. Keep your Seeking Name private. Traditionally, these are shared with very few people, if at all.

Write about your meditation in your journal. Explore how the Wilderness in your visualization reflects your experience of Wilderness in your journey. Does the landscape give you any fresh insights about the particular gifts and challenges of your Wilderness? (Explore the same questions with your nondominant hand.) Record your Seeking Name in your journal, if you wish. You may make drawings or paste artwork or photos around your Seeking Name that illustrate its meaning for you.

MEDITATION: THREE-PART INITIATION BREATH

The Sufi mystic Kabir calls God "the breath inside the breath." Breathing allows us to rest in What Is, and trust the process. This meditation will give you a tool to safely experience the whole cycle of Loss, Wilderness, and New Life through the natural rhythm of your own breath. Give yourself ten minutes minimum for this meditation.

Get comfortable, either sitting or lying down. Close your eyes and feel the support beneath you. Allow yourself to sink into, and receive, that support. Take several deep, slow breaths, allowing your belly to soften and relax, and then allow your breathing to begin to find its own natural rhythm. Follow the breath, in and out. When thoughts and feelings come, simply notice them and return to the breath.

Simply observe your breath, knowing that your body knows exactly how to breathe: when to exhale and release the old breath, when to rest between breaths, and when to inhale a new breath and start the cycle anew.

As you exhale, feel yourself releasing the old breath, letting go of what is finished.

In that moment between breaths, allow yourself to relax into the in-betweenness. Feel the spaciousness. Notice that when it is time for a new breath, your body simply breathes; there is no need to rush or force.

As you inhale, feel your body taking in new life, receiving it in this natural rhythm of letting go of the breath, resting, and taking in a new breath.

If you find yourself uncomfortable in that space between breaths (most of us are), simply allow the discomfort to be there. As you relax into the cycle, trusting more and more deeply that a new breath will always be there when it is time, allow yourself to play a little with the space between breaths. Trust it. Float in it. Allow it to expand a little. And keep noticing that the cycle has an integrity and rhythm of its own; there is always another breath, and another cycle, waiting to happen.

After you are done, notice if your discomfort with being between breaths has lessened. You can play with this breathing cycle any time; I like to do it at stoplights to slow myself down.

Learning to trust—during the microcycle of breathing—that a new cycle always arises from the space between breaths teaches us about the macrocycles of our lives and allows us to trust Wilderness, that time between the outbreath of our old lives and the inbreath of our lives-to-be.

6
Seeking Solitude, Learning from Elders

Imagine that you are a tribal initiate in another place and time. You have been ripped away from friends and family at the beginning of your initiation. Your head has been shorn, your familiar clothes and possessions removed, your name changed. The comfortable container of your old life has shattered, little of it through your own powers of choice and will. You feel frightened, confused, and strangely excited.

You are in the liminal stage, a threshold dweller, permanently bereft of your old life. Your life-to-come is still unknown. You are suspended in the utter mystery of it all.

Your tribe deeply cares about you. They know the power of the transformational forces, and they wish you success in this initiation—both for you and for the regeneration and renewal of their own communal lives. Your tribe knows they must give you two things absolutely necessary for this success: one is the presence, wisdom, and containing power of elders, and the other is solitude.

As both a seasoned initiate and an "elder" who has midwifed many others through initiations, I wish that you could be lovingly held in such a tribe. Chances are, you aren't. If you're like me, the ocean that you swim in is a technological, fast-paced culture that places little value on community, relationships, and the transformative power of the Sacred.

So how do you ensure that you receive both of these necessary ingredients? Your own psyche will ensure that you get solitude. As you will see in this chapter, the emotional withdrawal and depression that is common at this time occurs because some deeper and wiser part of yourself knows that you need time away, even if you do not consciously choose it.

Finding an elder in order to benefit from his or her wisdom and presence can be more of a challenge. However, as you will also see in this chapter, elders are all around us in many forms. They may not have the staff and long grey beard of a Gandalf, or stand tall in the special ceremonial garb of a tribal elder. In our culture, they often go unannounced and unnoticed, shopping at your grocery store and driving station wagons. You will learn what to look for in an elder and get some ideas on how to find one.

SOLITUDE CALLS

Whether or not you look for it in this Wilderness stage, solitude will find you.

My client Anita "had it made." At age fifty, as the president of her own small marketing firm, she had traveled around the country, spent weekends in her country cabin, and enjoyed the best wines and the latest fashions. As a single woman, she loved her freedom and her friends. Life was very good until she discovered, to her complete horror, that her bookkeeper had been embezzling from her accounts.

Anita did her best to undo the damage of four years of shady bookkeeping, but it was too late. Her clients deserted her, and Anita had to declare bankruptcy. Her dream world shattered. Feeling deeply betrayed by longtime business associates, she had sought help from me in order to fix things quickly and efficiently so that she could get back in control right away. She found, however, that her soul was calling her in an entirely different direction. Now, instead of trying to pick up the pieces and force them to fit back together as they had been (or "doing the Humpty Dumpty," as Anita wryly called it), she decided to give herself some time to grieve over the end of an old way of life and gestate a new one.

So when I asked how this particular week had gone, Anita sighed and settled more deeply into the chair opposite me. I knew she had been looking forward to spending the weekend that had just passed with a group of good friends at her cabin.

"It wasn't at all what I expected. Friday night, when we were sitting around dinner and chatting, I suddenly realized I felt like I was on a different planet than the rest of them. Actually, a different universe. There they were chatting about this and that in their lives, and all I was hearing was 'yada yada yada yada.'"

I asked her what she did, and she lifted her eyebrows in response. "I was stumped at first. Here I was, the charming hostess. I could feel one part of me trying to do the Humpty Dumpty and talk like they were talking, but the rest of me just didn't have the energy. I excused myself from the table and stepped out on the deck. It wasn't enough. My feet just wanted to keep going, so I walked down the dirt road a little ways in the moonlight.

"I've never done that before, been out like that by myself at night. I'm not used to keeping my own company. I've spent my life working all the time and filling any available gaps with dinner parties and dates, or reading when I'm by myself. But I just kept walking. Here I was alone, in this immense silence and darkness. Some part of me was waking up that had been curled up in a corner of myself for a very long time."

To her astonishment, Anita went back to the group and announced she needed to spend most of the weekend by herself. While the others went shopping, Anita walked the dirt roads around her cabin. "I found that the more I was by myself, the more I wanted solitude. Out there on those roads, I didn't have to hold onto that old me any more. I could just *be*, for maybe the first time in my life. I could feel me shedding my old story and my old life. During those walks, I didn't have to be the Anita that was in charge, in control, always barreling ahead with the newest five-year plan."

When Anita returned to the city, her hunger for solitude grew. She lost interest in business gossip and high-fashion magazines. She found herself turning down invitations to the theater and dinner. "Some friends were just fine with this quieter, more introspective me. I found I could spend time with them, even though I turned them down sometimes, too. The other ones, though, fell totally left by the wayside. I wasn't interested in social chatter any more, and they weren't interested in a me who didn't want to sit around and chat."

As the weeks went on, Anita sometimes became afraid that she would want to be alone like this for the rest of her life. "None of my five- or ten-year plans ever included messing around with watercolors by myself on a Friday night or walking alone down an empty road. I didn't want to become hermetically sealed inside my own life!"

I reassured her that the need for solitude was very much a part of the stage she was in, and that she really wouldn't end up an eccentric recluse. I told her that her craving for solitude would lessen over time, and that at some point she would have renewed interest in rejoining the world, though not in the ways she had previously done.

Some of you, like Anita, follow your feet into solitude. Others of you may be drawn unwillingly into another kind of solitude, the enforced solitude of depression, very common at this stage. Depression is the movement of the soul going downward and inward. During depression, we isolate, crawling under the covers of our life, unconsciously mimicking the pattern of ancient rites where the initiate was put into forced solitude in caves, special huts, or wilderness places. The self-isolation that comes with depression opens us to making internal changes, opens us to internal guidance in the forms of dreams, voices, and visions. This depth of internal work is simply not possible when we are eyeball-deep in the extroverted rounds of everyday life. It has often been my experience that the more an initiate resists this going downward and inward, the worse the depression becomes; it is as if our soul will take us there, willingly or not. So the more we consciously give ourselves the gift of solitude, the less we will suffer.

In our feel-good culture, initiates are often medicated out of this sort of depression, which can abort the profound changes that are taking place. That being said, though, it is very important for me to state that medication *does* have its proper place. If your depression is prolonged and severe, if it totally incapacitates you or leaves you feeling actively suicidal, medication can be a great help. Sometimes, depression robs people of the vital energy they need to move through the stages of initiation, and in these cases, antidepressant medication should be an option.

Why Solitude?

We must cultivate a willingness to invade our own privacy in Wilderness. For many of us, this willingness rubs against our twenty-first-century urban grain: How can we spend "useless" time by ourselves when there is always that errand to run, those children to feed, that business deadline looming, that growing pile of dirty laundry in the bathroom? Our lives seem to be purposefully constructed to override any pull toward an inner life.

And yet, in Wilderness, we must be willing to follow the pull of that tide to go inward for three main reasons:

• **Rest and repair.** Medical researchers have coined the term "conservation reaction" to describe how children who have been severely burned will self-isolate while healing, literally or figuratively drawing the covers up around themselves. This conservation reaction is self-protective and self-healing, a way of withdrawing to allow the body and spirit to re-form into a new whole. After trauma, we, too, go through a conservation reaction, even if we have no wounds to show on the outside. We need time, and rest, and isolation for the kind of deep healing to take place that is needed after our lives shatter. This may take months, or even years, depending both upon the severity of the trauma and upon our own constitutional makeup. Learn to shepherd your time and energy wisely. I often need to explain this to clients and workshop participants who have been through a devastating emotional trauma and don't understand why they are still so tired a year later. I tell them to imagine what it would be like if their bodies had suffered from an illness or physical trauma as large as the one that broke their hearts. They usually respond by saying that they would be much more gentle and compassionate with themselves about the length of recuperation time. Well then, I say, your heart and soul need that same amount of recuperation and care. Our culture gives much more credence to blows to the body than blows to the soul. Our psyches, though, know there is no difference. Give yourself the gift of rest and renewal during this time. Know that your strength, your energy, and your interest in the things of this world will return in time, and far more deeply and completely, if you give yourself time. One of my favorite sayings is "Reculer pour mieux sauter," which is a French saying that tells of the importance of drawing back in order to jump farther. Your leap back into life will occur much more effortlessly and joyfully if you can now give yourself the gift of drawing back, like a cat drawing backward and pausing before making a great leap forward.

• **Listening to self.** "Listen. Make a way for yourself inside yourself," writes Rumi, a twelfth-century Sufi mystic. We run ourselves ragged spending much of our lives listening to the radio, our boss, the television, our partner, our children, our stockbroker, our friends, our coworkers. We drive ourselves crazy trying to make sure all the voices in our head—the internal committee of parents, teachers, church, and so forth—are happy with us and approve of our lives. Often it is not until we have been blindsided by trauma, in Wilderness time, that we give ourselves the immense gift of listening to our own hearts and souls in any extended way. It is often all those other voices that keep us caught up in daily habits that obscure or obliterate our own authentic needs, until we can no longer hear the song only our soul can sing, or see the utter glory of the world around us. Solitude offers us the opportunity to recalibrate our lives, to rediscover that True North that points us to a deeply authentic expression of our spirits. "Long ago the word 'alone' was treated as two words, 'all one,'" Jungian analyst Clarissa Pinkola Estes writes in Women Who Run with the Wolves. "That is precisely the goal of solitude, to be all one. Solitude is not an absence of energy or action, as some believe, but is rather a boon of wild provisions transmitted to us from the soul. In ancient times, purposeful solitude was used as an oracle, as a way of listening to the inner self to solicit advice and guidance otherwise impossible to hear in the din of daily life." Many of the practices you will be reading about in the next chapters—visioning, dream tending, asking Big Questions, cultivating

Beginner's Mind—require solitude. Initiation carries us into the under-world of Dis; it takes time and solitude to mine this underworld of the gold of its immense wisdom to carry back with us into the daylight of our post-initiation lives. As we cultivate our capacity to be alone, "all one," we also cultivate our ability to listen to the stirrings of our hearts, the voices of our deepest needs and longings.

• **Communion with Spirit.** Whatever your term is for that larger Reality—God, Spirit, Source, Higher Power—that divine Presence is often most deeply apprehended in silence, receptivity, and solitude. It is said that Rabbi Nachman of Bratzlav made this prayer every morning of his life: "God grant me the ability to be alone. May it be my custom to go outdoors each day among the trees and the grasses, among all growing things, and there may I be alone, and enter into prayer with the one I belong to." The Sufi poet Kabir sings, "My inside, listen to me, the great-est Spirit, the Teacher, is near. Wake up, wake up!" When we are alone, it is easier to open to Spirit, and we find the Teacher is everywhere: in the prayer of our hearts and souls, in the rough bark of a pine tree we lean against, in the wind that calls our name. For some, this is a time to dig more deeply into their own spiritual tradition; for others, it is a time to step outside their known spiritual practices and allow themselves to find the Teacher in unaccustomed ways and places. Mary, a lapsed-and-returned Catholic, found no solace in the rosary or the Mass after the sud-den loss of both parents in a plane crash. I asked her when she felt most centered, and after careful thought she responded that it was with her daily morning run. I suggested to her that she allow her run to become a form of prayer, to let her body be with God around Green Lake, since her heart had run out of words. Do what most connects you with Spirit, whether that is lighting a candle and praying, or windsurfing. Spiritual tra-ditions the world over counsel disciples to withdraw, whether for twenty minutes, a day, or a lifetime, to better hear the still small voice within, to cultivate listening deeply to Spirit in the present moment. Most of us, as a friend once told me, practice EMT (emergency medical technician) listen-ing, meaning that we listen to Spirit only in times of emergency. This time in Wilderness spent learning to practice deep listening, both to ourselves and to God, prepares us for a richer future where we will be more open to guidance and spiritual support at any time, for anything.

Solitude also allows us to continue the self-care and self-nurturing that we began cultivating in the Loss stage. This self-caring must preclude chores and busywork. I once had a client who, after I had given him the assignment to spend an evening by himself, returned to say that it didn't feel any different. A little suspicious, I asked him how he had spent his time alone. He told me he had turned on the radio and paid bills!

This time alone is set-apart time. Time for you and your soul. Even if you can afford only half an hour, turn off the phone and the TV. Let the kids and the partner know that this is uninterruptible, sacred time. (If your children are too young, find someone to care for them during this time, or do it when they are asleep.) Take a walk, write in your journal, sit under a tree and listen to what it says to you, watch the clouds make patterns in the sky. Listen to your heart and soul. Continue your grieving work as needed. Hold your own hand. Pray and meditate. Ask yourself questions about what is happening in your life without judgment, shame, or blame. Learn to tell the truth to yourself, about yourself.

One time deep in my illness, I spent an entire slow evening giving myself a manicure and a pedicure, something I had never done before. Exhausted as I was, I consciously groomed myself as a tangible expression of self-care and compassion. Deeply spiritual it wasn't, but healing it was. I spent much of my time, alone and with others, in "spiritual" activity. I needed, at that time, to learn to care for my body and learn to see that as spiritual practice.

Self-care at this time also means finding and creating routines that are grounding and containing, such as small rituals to begin the morning or end the evening, a nightly bath, or meditatively fixing dinner. Keep what works from your old life. Find those activities that can creatively hold your attention and remind you of a part of you that is continuous and unchanging even in the midst of such upheaval. Connect with the part of you that still does certain things every day, that has a track record, a part of you—however small—

that does *not* feel uncertain and in-between. Don't retreat into that part, but do draw upon its stabilizing influence.

FINDING ELDERS

Ancient initiates did not undergo their transformational journey alone. We're simply not wired to do this deep work by ourselves.

Since the dawn of humankind, there have always been those who have had the capacity, the wisdom, and the calling to hold space for others who are deep in the throes of initiation. These women and men help create a psychic container for the strong transformative energies of Wilderness time and offer their wisdom and guidance as needed. We still have them among us today, although they are not often called elder, medicine person, priestess, or shaman.

I feel that I owe the "success" of any initiation I've undergone to the presence (sometimes comforting, sometimes more than a little disturbing!) of an elder. The initiation I underwent that took many more years to move through than need be—the loss of my musical career through tendinitis—was the one in which I had no elder to guide me, and in which I did not even know the necessity of having one. In all my other initiations, I was aided by elders: psychotherapists, spiritual directors, teachers, wise friends.

"When you are in the throes of initiation, there are not a whole lot of people you can talk to about it," says Barbara Fischer, a psychotherapist who has suffered for years from fibromyalgia and is a revered elder herself. "It's lonely; everyone has ideas of what you should do; they are full of solutions because they are so afraid of *your* situation. You run into other people's fears big time if they haven't been through this stage themselves. Trouble is, your life's not 'solvable' in any way. It's so important to find people who know, really know, what it's like to wander around in the dark."

What makes an elder? First and foremost, elders by any name have been "around the block" enough times themselves to understand the powerful transformative process of life/death/rebirth. A true elder *won't*:

- Rush you through your Wilderness time
- Try to fix or solve you or your life

- Have an investment in the outcome of your journey (the people we most love often have the greatest stakes in the way our lives turn out)
- Take the position that something is "wrong" with you
- Reduce you to a diagnostic label

Rather, a true elder *will*:

- Be comfortable with uncertainties, ambiguities, and the unknown
- Have been through enough initiations of his or her own to deeply trust the process
- Discern between "normal" depression and depression that breeds on itself in an unhealthy way
- Hold nonjudgmental space for all that you think and feel
- Be deeply grounded spiritually (an elder doesn't have to believe the same things you do, but must be open and supportive of your own exploration and beliefs)
- Have confidence in your ability to move through your initiation, and will support your ability to do so
- Challenge you on your beliefs and assumptions when appropriate

An elder will be wise. Wisdom is a much harder thing to find in our culture than knowledge, and an even harder concept to define. We value knowledge—facts and conceptual understanding—and must have it to get through our everyday lives and make a living. But what we are in desperate need of is wisdom, which will help us actually "make" a life. In *Essential Spirituality*, Roger Walsh writes:

> *Wisdom is deep understanding and practical skill in the central issues of life, especially existential and spiritual issues. Existential issues are those crucial and universal concerns all of us face simply because we are human. They include finding meaning and purpose in our lives; managing relationship and aloneness; acknowledging our limits and smallness in a universe vast beyond comprehension; living in inevitable uncertainty and*

mystery; and dealing with sickness, suffering, and death. A person who has developed deep insights into these issues—and skills for dealing with them— is wise indeed.

One of the greatest gifts an elder can give you is that he or she "gets" what you're going through. An elder will understand your need to stay in Wilderness for as long as it takes.

I once wrote an article on Wilderness entitled "Don't Get Over It" for a Seattle journal. It wasn't my choice of title; the editor liked its inflammatory quality. I expected to get negative feedback about my suggestion to let the process take the time it takes. Instead, I was flooded with letters and e-mail thanking me for permission to slow down and honor the process. The article took off, circling the globe several times; I received letters and e-mail from people in Switzerland, South Africa, and Hong Kong for five years. It touched a real nerve and highlighted for me the absolute necessity to have elders who are "permission givers" in this way.

An elder is someone who, in the words of psychotherapist Karlfried Graf Durkheim, will faithfully help those in the initiation process to *risk themselves*, "so that they may endure the suffering and pass courageously through it, thus making of it a raft that leads to the far shore." That elder could be a pastor or priest, a coach, a spiritual director. She, or he, could be a therapist; in my experience, transpersonal therapists and Jungian analysts, as a whole, are most familiar with this territory.

Finally, an elder might be a trusted friend—if, and only if, that friend has no vested interest in a particular outcome. One of the elders whom I am most grateful for is just that: Barbara, a longtime friend and deeply spiritual wise woman. Over the years, Barbara has "eldered" me through divorce and life-threatening illness. She has the extraordinary capacity to be deeply caring, but at the same time she sees the Big Picture and is unafraid to compassionately ask me those disturbing Big Questions.

Be careful, though, if you look to a friend for "eldering." Friends tend to encourage the old self to struggle to survive; after all, that's the one they've known and loved all these years. Anita discovered that many of her friends turned away from her when she began asking the Big Questions about her life. She felt hurt, angry, and rejected until she realized that their turning away from her was more about their own anxieties over living an unexamined life than it was about her.

Often the best way to find an elder is to ask someone else who has been through an initiation. If you are connected with a spiritual organization, ask other members. If you look for a therapist, coach, or spiritual director, interview them. Most are willing to talk with you on the phone for ten minutes or so, enough time for you to get an initial impression. Don't be afraid to ask them hard questions: "Have you worked before with trauma as a catalyst for transformation? Have you worked with and experienced in your own life a deep literal or metaphorical death and rebirth? How comfortable are you with ambiguity, paradox, and not knowing? How do you decide to medicate someone who's depressed? How do you work with dreams?"

You may find one therapist you immediately take to, or you may need to have a first session with several different ones to get a better feel for how they work. Trust your intuition here. It is ultimately the relationship itself that heals, the quality of the connection between the two of you. This doesn't mean that you'd like your therapist for your best friend. But it does mean that you trust this person's integrity and wisdom, you feel his or her caring, and some deeper, nonrational part of you says Yes to this therapist as your guide.

If all this feels overwhelming, stop for a moment and take a breath. Enlist the help of a partner or friend to do the sleuthing for you. Pray for a mentor to show up. Be willing for this elder to look like nothing you would have consciously chosen. I once worked with an elder who was an overweight, very direct Hawaiian kahuna. He didn't hold my hand, literally or metaphorically. He didn't say kind or comforting words, or reassure me that I'd get through the initiation process intact. He broke all my internal rules for how my "ideal elder" would look or behave. Puni was nothing like anything I ever thought I wanted, but he was *exactly* what I needed at the time.

If you live in a rural area where finding an elder may seem impossible, know that elders are alive and thriving in many books. You may find their wisdom in literature such as *The Hobbit*. Elders appear in myths, tribal stories, and fairy tales the world over. You can also find contemporary elders in current psychospiritual books on the market. Take yourself to a library or bookstore for a couple of hours, ask for guidance, and notice which books draw you in, inspire you, give you strength and courage and hope. You can find some recommended reading at the end of this book.

You may also find "spiritual elders" through prayer and guided imagery. If you have a spiritual figure you already connect with—Jesus, the Buddha, Kuan Yin—create a sacred inner space through guided imagery, invite your chosen elder in to answer your questions and offer guidance (see the Interlude at the end of Chapter Four).

Finally, we all carry an "inner elder," a Wise Self who knows us better than we can ever consciously know ourselves. You may have met this inner elder if you worked with the guided imagery from Interlude Four. One of the great gifts, I believe, of the process of initiation is to discover, and learn to trust, this Wise Self within.

You will traverse much of your Wilderness in solitude. "Going within" is a necessary part of the process. But this does not mean that assistance and guidance are not available to you. Seek out the wisdom of an elder to comfort you and support you on your journey. They have been on similar journeys; they *know*.

Interlude Six

GOD-BATHING

David Steindl-Rast, a Benedictine monk, calls being in silence and solitude "God-bathing." God-bathing is wonderful when we are feeling empty or when we need help letting go and allowing our lives to be carried and cared for by God.

Find a time when you will be undisturbed for ten to twenty minutes. Settle yourself in a cozy and comfortable rocking chair, armchair, or couch. Bring to your mind and heart an image, or a feeling, of the Divine as a tender Mother. Ask this Mother to hold you and comfort you. Wrap your arms around yourself gently, or hold your hands softly over your heart. Begin to rock softly, as you are being held in the arms of the Mother. Open your body and your heart to this Mother's infinite nurturing and unconditional love.

Simply allow yourself to *receive*. Some people find it comforting to sing a childhood lullaby or a hymn or chant, or simply to "hear" it with their inner ears. Feel the comfort spreading into every cell of your body; allow your heart to dilate open wide to receive this nurturing. You may find yourself crying as if you were a small child, or simply being in silence. Continue for as long as you like; when you are ready to "come back," thank this Mother for Her care, ask for this care to continue on, and allow yourself to slowly and gently return to the room, bringing back with you the deep sense of comfort and love.

PRAYER STICK

Traditional cultures around the world have often decorated sticks for particular intentions: prayers, healing, gratitude, hunting, and working with the powers of nature. Creating a prayer stick can give a tangible form to your prayers and intentions. You will need:

- A stick, dowel, or slender tree branch approximately 18 inches long
- A piece of paper about 3 inches square, and a pen (or colored pens) for writing your prayer or intention
- Tape or stickers to seal the paper
- Several different colors of yarn or ribbons for wrapping around your prayer stick
- Any talismans, beads, stones, feathers, or dried herbs that you would like to add to the stick

Write your intention or prayer on the paper, wrap it around the prayer stick close to the top, and seal it with tape or stickers. With your first yarn or ribbon color, hold the tail pointing down next to the stick, and begin to wrap the yarn around the stick from the top down, eventually covering the yarn tail.

When you wish to change yarn or ribbon colors, place the tail of the second color next to the tail of the first color. Wrap the second color down the stick until you have covered both tails. You may either wrap until the bottom of the stick, or leave several inches bare at the bottom to plant your prayer stick in the ground in the traditional way. When you have wrapped as far down as you want to go, tie several knots in the yarn or ribbon and trim the end.

As you wrap, hold your intention or prayer in your heart; imagine wrapping the stick with your prayer. You can experiment with wrapping several different colors at the same time. If you wish, you can tie a talisman, stone, feather, or dried herb to an additional piece of yarn, and tie the other end of the yarn to the top of your prayer stick so that the object hangs from the top of the stick.

When you are done, you can plant your prayer stick in the ground with additional prayers, or place the prayer stick on your altar or some other special place. Try meditating in front of your altar holding your prayer stick.

ALTAR UPDATE

Take some time to sit with your altar. What does your altar say to you, with its colors and arrangement of objects? Does this current arrangement speak clearly to your heart and soul, or does your altar need clearing and the addition of new objects to reflect your life now?

If you decide that your altar needs to change, clear it off completely and clean it, being aware as you do so that you are symbolically clearing out your life as well. Sit before your empty altar and reflect on what you need at this point. What is your current intention for your altar: Courage? Faith? Healing? Guidance? Your intention will guide the ongoing creation, and re-creation, of your altar. What colors might reflect your current intention? What objects or icons? Would you like a vessel (a beautiful cup or bowl) for holding your written intentions, affirmations, or prayers?

Cultivate your "second attention" to be looking for objects for your altar. I find sacred objects in beach walks, secondhand stores, bookstores, and walks around my neighborhood. Rather than looking for something in particular, play with staying open to what is "looking" for you. Allow yourself to be found!

7
Letting Go: Surrender

Let me tell you my favorite teaching story, one that I hope to continue learning for the rest of my life:

A woman is being pursued by a terrible monster. She reaches a cliff, and knows her only hope is to jump. Falling, falling, she sees a root sticking out from the cliffside and grabs it. The root stops her fall, but the earth around it crumbles, and she knows the root will soon pull free from the cliff.

In desperation, she calls out, "Help! Help! Is there anyone up there that can help me? Help!"

A voice, calm and reassuring, answers, "I am here. I can help you."

"Who are you?" shouts the woman.

"I am God, your Beloved."

"Please, please, save me! Tell me what to do!"

God answers, "Let go."

The woman looks up in disbelief, looks down at the great space beneath her, then looks up once more, and calls, "Is there anyone else up there?"

TRANSFORMATION THROUGH SUBTRACTION

When you are sojourning in Wilderness, you are practicing transformation through subtraction. You know what you've lost. What you will gain from this process—and there will be many gifts—is still unknown. You may grieve over the past or rage about its loss, but nothing will bring it back.

Your future seems perhaps more unknown now than at any other time in your life tha you can recall. We usually project our future based upon our past: our self-concepts, beliefs, relationships. In Wilderness, many of those markers of our life as we know it are gone. The future may be total mystery: not just our "outer" future, the events of our lives, but our "inner" future—the "who" that will be subjectively experiencing those events. Mystery brings with it a pervasive sense of insecurity.

"That insecurity comes because normally we are in a state of being spread out in time," David Spangler, author of *Blessings*, told me in an interview. "Part of us is in the past, part in the present, part in the future. All of these parts define who we are and what we do. But when I am in Wilderness, it's as if the past and future parts of our time-bodies get lopped off. We feel amputated." However, Spangler explains, we aren't lopped off from the present: "Time has collapsed into the present moment, which all spiritual and mystical disciplines say is where it should be anyway. If I can consciously turn my attention to fully being in the present moment and whatever that moment offers me, that goes a long way toward diminishing the insecurity I feel, and reconnects me with my own wisdom and creative energy."

Fully being in the present moment probably doesn't feel very inviting. The present moment of your Wilderness life may not feel particularly creative or special. "The present moment is about the last place in the world I want to be right now," my client Lisa told me, weeping. Lisa had lost her home, her belongings, and her two dogs in a terrible fire. When we are feeling the utter devastation of our loss, which we will continue to feel in waves throughout much of Wilderness, the present moment doesn't feel so good; it has no welcome mat.

This chapter is not about trying to make you feel excited or happy to be in the present. I remember crawling out of my house one particularly bad morning, exhausted and depressed from months of chronic fatigue syndrome, to have a latte at Starbucks just for the sake of getting out of the house. I had no sooner sunk into an armchair than an acquaintance who knew I was very ill recognized me. She sat down next to me and asked how I was doing. I told her the truth: awful.

She sighed, looked deep into my eyes, and actually told me how fortunate I was to be so ill, how illness brings us all into the present moment. I was stunned at her insensitivity to how painful and unwelcome the present moment was for me at that point. She glanced at her watch, rose to go, laid a hand on my arm and chirped, "Remember: the past is a memory, the future a dream. What you have now is this moment, a true gift. That's why it's called 'the present.'"

If I had had the strength, I would have hit her. Her glibness outraged me. So I'm not going to say the same thing to you.

The present moment, in Wilderness, is often not a pleasant place. Staying in the present is challenging when life hurts or is deeply uncertain. However, if you can learn to be "in" it, you will begin to reap its profound gifts: healing, extraordinary insights, flowering of self-compassion, peace of mind and heart, and a joy that is unattached to any particular person or event. Surrender may not transform your outer circumstances, at least not immediately. Surrender, however, instantly transforms *you*.

A woman once traveled a great distance through the jungle to ask the Buddha for advice and guidance. Kneeling before him as he meditated, she said, "Oh great awakened One, please help me. I am so hungry. I have no food, and no money for food. Please, what shall I do?"

After a moment of silence, the Buddha opened his eyes, gazed at her with great compassion, and said softly, "Fast."

"The difference between starving and fasting is surrender," says Barbara Fischer, a psychotherapist who suffers severe chronic pain from fibromyalgia. "It's about taking responsibility for where you are and saying, 'I'll stop spending my energy fighting this thing, whether "this thing" is pain, loss, or death. I'll open myself fully to it and become curious about what it has to offer me.' We usually have to try everything else first, until there is no other alternative left. When the Sacred tells us to let go, we say, 'Do you have any other ideas?' Surrender is about making open space, that crack in the cosmic egg, for the Sacred, for new life, to pour through."

The great therapist and wise man Carl Jung echoed the Buddha's words and Fischer's sentiments when he once advised a patient, "If you find you're falling, jump."

Surrender is the ultimate dirty word in our control-crazy culture, smacking of defeat and failure, of handing ourselves over to the "enemy," of losing our integrity or even our life. Surrender is not, however, about giving up or giving in. The Latin root of "surrender" means to "give back." In surrender, we are simply giving back to God what was not ours in the first place, the ultimate control of our life.

The major spiritual traditions celebrate surrender as a cornerstone of a deeply lived spiritual life. As Wayne Muller writes in *Sabbath: Restoring the Sacred Rhythm of Rest*, "Jesus' most poignant prayer—prayed when he knew he was soon to die—was simply this: 'Thy will be done.' This is not defeat or resignation, but astonishing faith that there are spiritual forces that will bear him up, regardless of the outcome. Often in our striving for a particular result, we are not willing to be surprised by a healing we cannot imagine. Paradoxically, it is often cowardice that makes us hold on to our own small solutions; it takes infinitely more courage to surrender."

Surrender is the ultimate Yes to the present moment of our lives, whatever that holds for us, and Yes to a Greater Power that holds us as we move through our lives, moment by moment.

SURRENDER TO WHAT IS

When faced with the aftermath of trauma, most of us spend a great deal of energy resisting What Is. In surrender, we are asked to name the particulars of our lives as they are this moment: *this* cancer, *this* aching grief for a lost partner, *this* joblessness. By ceasing to resist What Is, we stop running from our lives and stand still long enough for a deeper wisdom to emerge, for God to find us through prayer, meditation, gardening, dreaming. It is only by surrendering in the Wilderness that we can receive new learning, hope, and possibilities. Surrender is a softening, a recognition that we can't do this transition alone. Surrender is a call for spiritual help and guidance, a cry for our own passionate and authentic life to find us.

Diana Nares vividly remembers that the first time she had to learn about surrender was after her child Emilio was diagnosed with leukemia: "For a while I actually thought things would change. 'He really doesn't have leukemia! I'm going to wake up from this nightmare and everything is going to be just like it was before.' Well, I finally got it that I couldn't 'fix' the situation, make it be what I desperately wanted it to be. I had to learn how to surrender. I had to learn how to surrender every day to the reality of Emilio's disease and his suffering. So much that happens to us is out of our direct control. I now realize that I have to surrender to the events of my life. It is only by doing so that I can get through each day."

This surrendering simply means saying Yes, a deep and heartfelt Yes, to the present moment. Surrendering is about bringing full attention to What Is, choosing not to focus on what has been, or should be. It is the willing "jump," naked and undefended, into the truth of What Is Now. Surrendering doesn't mean being happy about your life or thanking God for What Is, though that may ultimately come. It doesn't mean not doing anything to change the situation. It doesn't mean giving up, helplessly waiting for God to rescue you from your misery. Surrendering, for Diane, did not mean giving up on Emilio's treatment. It meant pursuing every possible cure, while realizing she was not in ultimate control of the outcome. It meant holding Emilio's hand during treatment and opening her heart to his suffering, while knowing she couldn't take it away. It meant surrendering the illusion that she could "make" Emilio better through sheer force of her will, or through the right number or kinds of prayers, or the next miracle drug.

Surrender means looking at the present reality of your life with eyes and heart wide open. It means letting go of an ultimate particular outcome while doing what we can in the present. This kind of surrender is not passive or wimpy; on the contrary, it is consciously chosen and takes great courage. Surrender can break our hearts open to unexpected love and compassion, once we let go of trying to fix things or to make life unfold according to our demands. A therapist friend of mine, Beth Fisher, looks at surrender in another way. She learned about surrendering to the present moment in the trenches: she has been through breast cancer twice. Beth, whose Buddhist practices carried her through some very dark times, sees surrender simply as the ability *to send love to whatever is happening in your life.*

Surrender doesn't change our outer circumstances, but it transforms our relationship with those circumstances. My client Amanda's lifelong dream had always been to be a mother. As a child she played with dolls and dreamed of the time when she would have four children of her own. Amanda and her husband spent a difficult three years working with an infertility clinic in order to realize her dream. She became pregnant twice; she miscarried twice. Amanda's doctor finally told her it would be dangerous for her to become pregnant again. Months later Amanda was still devastated and still fighting both the doctor and her husband. One afternoon, exhausted from a fight with her husband over whether to try again, Amanda collapsed on her couch and cried herself to sleep.

She woke up in the early evening. "Something had shifted, I'm not sure what," she told me at our next session. "All that fight had gone out of me. I finally got it, *really* got it, that I would never bear children of my own. The pain was more than I thought I could bear. How could I even live if I couldn't have my own children? Then, from somewhere deep inside of me, a very calm voice said, 'Amanda, this IS your life.' It startled me right out of my tears. I sat up and realized, yes, this *is* my life. I am a childless woman who has done everything I could to bear a child. This is not what I want. But this is what I have."

Amanda felt a measure of peace she hadn't felt in years. She sat there in the deepening darkness, surprised at the power of acknowledging What Is. "All my senses were heightened. I think it was the first time I had been in the present moment since we started infertility treatment. I had spent the last three years willing my way into a future with babies. I felt this space in my chest getting bigger and softer," she recalls.

Amanda became aware of being part of a lineage going back to the beginning of time, of women who had lost their babies through war, or famine, or disease. "I don't know quite how to say it, but surrendering to the reality of being childless, instead of fighting it tooth and nail, opened my heart to a much larger reality, of all these other women who had experienced such loss,"

Amanda said. "I realized I wasn't alone, and that I wasn't special. I know that sounds funny, but it was immensely comforting and healing. I thought, 'This is what happens in life. We are all deeply wounded, one way or the other. This is my wound, just like it has been for millions of women before me. I can keep fighting it, which just keeps ripping the wound wide open, or I can surrender to the reality of it, and start the healing.'"

Grace and healing occur when we step out of our own way and stop straining to force life to bend to our will. Letting go through surrender creates an opening in our hearts and souls through which the balm of grace and healing may begin to flow. Rainer Maria Rilke, a German poet who was a contemporary of Carl Jung's, took Jung's saying about choosing to jump and extended it another poetic step: "Whoever lets go in his fall, dives into the Source and is healed."

RESISTANCE TO SURRENDER

Few of us have developed the capacity to stay in the surrendered, wide-open space of the present moment. Our culture, the ocean we swim in, has dedicated itself to the ideals of control and mastery. Switch on the television, and ads will promise that if you wear the right deodorant, rinse with the right mouthwash, and drive the right car, you will be eternally happy, attractive, and popular. You can sign up for weekend courses that promise that your life will be utterly and unalterably changed in 48 hours. Take a trip to the drugstore: Bright boxes and packages offer us total happiness through the whitest smile, the most brilliant hair color. Books and tapes guarantee that if you follow their easy three-step program you'll lose weight or meet your perfect soul mate.

This illusion of control extends even to our spiritual lives. Many spiritual teachings, from New Age to fundamentalist, tell us if we only say the right affirmation the right number of times, or the right prayer in the right way, our lives will be abundant, worry-free, and happy. Spiritual courses promise easy enlightenment in twenty-one days.

There is little in our culture that gives us permission to let go of trying so hard to make sure things come out the way we want them to, whether it's on the physical, emotional, or spiritual plane. When you mix that together with a very understandable reluctance to feel emotional pain, you end up with some pretty powerful resistance to letting go into the reality of the present moment and releasing outcomes.

I have often found that my resistance to surrender is very strong. I won't go there, or just plain can't. I'm reminded of the intense frustration of being at my best friend's farm as a child, trying to get their old mule Bertha to budge by pulling on her halter. It just doesn't work. When I try to *force* myself to surrender, I only add to my suffering. Surrendering is about *allowing*, not coercing.

Sometimes the present moment seems too painful. I'm scared. I already feel too helpless and battered by life to be willing to be vulnerable and open, even if only with myself. I resist by fleeing to the refrigerator, going slack-jawed before the TV, driving to the mall for a little retail therapy, flipping open my laptop for an hour or two of Websurfing.

When we are feeling deeply resistant to surrendering, for whatever reason, we can simply back up a step and open and soften to the resistance itself. I can extend compassion to myself for fleeing in fear from my own life. I can send love to my grinding teeth and my fear of an unknown future. And if I can't soften my heart, I can breathe and soften around the hardness and tightness I feel there (as in the Metta meditation from Interlude Three).

You might especially feel resistance to opening to the present moment if you know what you'll find there is depression. We might be afraid that opening to our feelings of depression is the same as drowning in them. Depression is a normal part of Wilderness time, a reasonable response to a descent into grief and not-knowing: The old spiritual tools don't work; the old emotional certainties are gone. For the most part, depression during Wilderness is not pathological; it's part of the process of being "dismembered" in order to be reborn.

A few of us may need to surrender only once. Most of us will need to make the choice to surrender tens or hundreds or thousands of times, over months or even years.

Amanda didn't remain in that wide-open surrendered space. She found herself falling back into fighting the reality of being childless, of wanting to twist the outcome in a different direction. Amanda realized she harbored a secret hope that surrender was a one-time event. She knew she was resisting the present moment when she tightened up, clenched her jaw, and stopped breathing. Amanda learned in her work with me to stop and breathe into the resistance, and send compassion to her struggle. "I could then remember sitting on that couch in the darkness, and think, 'If all those other women could work through this grief, then I can too. I can be soft with myself, and open my heart to my own life.'" Tears often followed, but they were healing tears, not ones of anger, frustration, and resistance.

Surrender to Spirit

Surrendering to the present moment brings us to the second, and even deeper, level of surrender. Most spiritual traditions emphasize the necessity of ultimate surrender to a larger Presence in whom we live and move and have our being. This second level is about a deeper letting go while trusting that the process, and the ultimate outcome, are held in the wide and loving arms of the Beloved.

"That open and surrendered space is in fact a mystical experience," teacher David Spangler told me. "You can find a source of courage and power and creativity in the present moment that you can always draw on, a rootedness in a universal Being. This open space is homologous with the spiritual experience, though when I've lost my partner or am worried if I can pay my rent, I may not see the present moment as being deeply spiritual. But if I can stay with the present moment and allow it to deepen me, to carry me beyond fear and anxiety to a place where I can surrender into that Being, then it can take me deep into spirituality."

I don't come to this level of surrender easily. Back in college my friends and I shook our fists at the stars, passionately reciting Dylan Thomas: "Do not go gentle into that good night/Rage, rage against the dying of the light." I had vowed then to go down fighting. I found myself still shaking my fist at God in September of 2001. The World Trade Center had collapsed, and so had my personal world. My dearest friend Gretchen, whom I passionately love, had just been diagnosed with cancer. I knew I needed to find a deeper level of surrender to Spirit, to trusting both the process and the outcome, but nothing in my life, or in my culture, showed me how to consciously open to this sort of surrender.

I searched for a practice to lead me into deeper surrender and discovered it in the five-times prayer, *Salat*, of the Sufi tradition. I learned to bow before the immense grace of What Is under the tutelage of a Sufi teacher. I added my own prayer to the postures: *Oh God, I surrender my mind to Your wisdom, my heart to Your love, my life to Your healing presence*. I found myself prostrating myself right into the boundless arms of the Beloved.

Nothing had changed on the outside: Gretchen still struggled with chemotherapy's devastation. The world still wrestled with terrorism. Women widowed that September morning gave birth to fatherless babies. I grieved for the women and children in Afghanistan, fumed over Americans' quiescence as our civil liberties were being chipped away. But my life opened up. The more I practiced surrendering it all to God's wisdom and care, the more I could open my heart to it all and surrender the ultimate outcome of everything back to where it belonged, in God's hands.

When I grew frightened about anthrax or chemical warfare, I prayed for the ability to let go and trust the larger unfolding. I held Gretchen's hand as the nurse pierced her skin with the chemotherapy needle and remembered to breathe, to soften and surrender to the present moment: a room of people suffering with cancer, an impersonal and overloaded medical system, nurses doing their best to dispense caring and hope as well as drugs. I began to viscerally understand Reinhold Niebuhr's Serenity Prayer: *God grant me the serenity to accept the things I cannot change, the courage to change the things I can, and the wisdom to know the difference*.

In surrender, we give back to God our demand to understand the Big Picture of why things happen the way they do. We give back our insistence that life behave a certain way in order for us to feel good and the mistaken belief that well-being depends on outside circumstances rather than our inner connection with the Source of all Life and Love. We release the desperate scrabbling at control. We unfetter our lives, and the life of the world around us, into Mystery, that wisdom which is beyond our capacity to understand.

Surrender isn't about not caring; it is about allowing ourselves to receive Divine Love *and* to love more wholeheartedly than we ever dreamed possible. This act of waking up to Divine love is the aim of all spiritual paths. Surrender graces us with the immutable joy of being fully present to life—not just the pain and suffering, but the love that connects us with family, friends, strangers. We surrender to all of Creation: the fragile beauty of a spiderweb illuminated by autumn sunlight, the sweet smell of a baby's head, the deep gratitude for a good meal shared. Surrender is the gate that swings wide open to the living heart of God.

Diane Nares is still practicing surrender several years after Emilio's death: "Every day, I ask for a lot of help. I pray and surrender to God: 'Please help me get through the pain when it rolls in and knocks me off my feet.' I surrender to the pain and fear. Little by little, I am comforted. I am reminded that I have felt the worst and I'm still alive. I can smile again, I am hopeful again, I can find beauty in nature again. I am receiving help."

Surrender is not a self-help tool guaranteeing that things go our way if we use the right affirmation or positive thinking. Surrender does open us up to trusting the wisdom of uncertainty, the ability to be flexible and open-hearted no matter what comes down the pike. In surrendering, we find a deeper seat of power and wisdom from which to act in our life according to our own true values and visions. Surrender frees us to act from our deepest core in the present moment, without losing precious energy fixating on a specific desirable outcome.

With surrender, we tap into something much greater than our own personal energy. We have moved into the force field of God, the "electromagnetic field of Love," as Sufi teacher Kabir Helminski says. Far more love and intelligence is available within this field than we can ever find within just ourselves. By letting go of resistance to what is, right now, we surrender to the present moment, the holy field of love and power. The present moment is our opening to God.

The first anniversary of the September 11 terrorist attacks has come and gone. My dear friend Gretchen is in remission. I am tempted to quit my Sufi prostrations, dismissing them as medicine for an acute ailment now cured.

However, I have learned to acknowledge the tremendous fragility of our world, and so I will continue Salat, knowing that my prostrations will ensure neither peace nor a "happy ending" for myself or anyone else. These prostrations simply remind me, breath after breath, to keep opening my heart wide to love and the wild adventure of living in these times. Jelaluddin Rumi, a twelfth-century Sufi mystic who also lived in wild times, wrote:

> *Gamble everything for love,*
> *if you're a true human being.*
> *Half-heartedness doesn't reach*
> *into majesty. You set out*
> *to find God, but then you keep*
> *stopping for long periods at mean-spirited roadhouses.*

Trauma shocks us out of half-heartedness. Surrender keeps us out of those mean-spirited roadhouses, and on the path of love.

Interlude Seven

We all learn in different ways. For those of us who are primarily visual, guided imagery seems to work best. For those of us who learn with our bodies, I offer here a way to physically learn surrender. I encourage even those of you who are not kinesthetic to try the second exercise because for something tough like surrender, allowing the body to participate can bring the learning and the healing to an entirely different level. The first exercise is a simple guided meditation. The second, Salat, is adapted from the Sufi/Muslim tradition.

SURRENDER MEDITATION

Sit comfortably in a place where you will be undisturbed for twenty minutes.

Close your eyes, take several deep breaths, soften your belly, your eyes, your tongue, your jaw. Breathe into your heart, allowing it to soften and open.

Imagine a being of Divine love and compassion standing before you: the Buddha, Jesus, Quan Yin, Mohammed, Krishna. Bring your hands together, palms up, as if you were holding something. Imagine holding whatever it is you wish to surrender in your cupped hands. Feel the weight of your grief, your fear of the future, your despair, the outcome of your illness, whatever it is that you wish to surrender.

Then offer your burden to the Divine Being.

Let whatever it is you're carrying go. Allow the Divine Being to take it, and hold it in infinite compassion, love, and wisdom. Notice what an immense relief it is to let it go into the hands of the Beloved. You no longer have to carry its weigh or be consumed with worry about its future. Let it go. Drop your hands into your lap, and allow yourself to be surrounded and filled with this love and compassion. Thank the Beloved and gently return to the room.

SALAT

Muslims pray by prostrating themselves in surrender to God five times a day, using the body to express adoration and gratitude. Thanks to Jamal Rahman, minister of the Interfaith Church in Seattle and a third-generation Sufi teacher, here are instructions for an amended form of Salat. (Many thanks to *Spirituality and Health* magazine, which gave permission for this explanation to be adapted here.) Rahman stresses that the most critical element is your sincerity; keep your attention on essence, not form. Far more important than the exact words or postures are the sincerity and humility with which you carry out the cycle. The basic cycle is as follows:

1. Stand in the presence of God.
2. Create sacred intentions by raising outstretched palms, symbolizing that for now you are putting the world behind you and are ushered into communion with Spirit.
3. Lower your hands and offer praise and thanksgiving to your Creator.
4. Bow in humility by bending at the waist and resting your hands on your knees.
5. Stand upright.
6. Prostrate yourself to God by gracefully dropping to your knees and pressing your forehead on the floor.
7. Draw back up and sit in a kneeling position.
8. Prostrate yourself to God again by touching your forehead to the floor.
9. Stand upright and repeat Steps 3 to 8.
10. This time, instead of standing up, kneel by sitting back on your heels.
11. Bring your body prayer to a close by turning your head to right and left, saying, "Peace and blessings to you." This greeting is intended for the two angels who accompany every human being, and also for the host of angels who congregate in spaces of sacredness and beauty.
12. Conclude prayers in the kneeling position by asking God for forgiveness, making supplications, and expressing gratitude.

Rahman says that among the countless blessings of body prayer practiced over time, three stand out:

- The dissolving of the rigidity of the ego. "One prostration of prayer to God frees you from a thousand prostrations to your ego," is a favorite saying among Islamic mystics.
- Prostration purifies the heart so that it becomes like a polished mirror in which Divinity is reflected.
- One becomes imbued with what the Quran calls "qurb," a nearness to the Beloved.

My own experience of practicing Salat after 9/11 and my dear friend's diagnosis of cancer is that I received all three blessings. In surrendering myself physically to God, I could let go of my demands for how my life should look, and what I was and wasn't willing to deal with. Practicing Salat opened my heart, time after time, allowing the loving presence of God to replace my fears and insecurities.

Encouraged by Jamal's insistence on essence, not form, I wrote my own prayer, which I substituted for the traditional Muslim prayers for each position. With each movement, I repeated, "Oh Divine Beloved: I surrender my mind to Your wisdom, my heart to Your love, my life to Your healing presence." Slowly, slowly, prostration after prostration, the prayer wore away my incessant demands for security. The prayer became part of my breath; I now find myself saying it in the morning before arising and when I find myself resisting That Which Is or engaging in some futile struggle for MY way.

Experiment with the traditional prayers, my prayer, or a prayer of your own. Rahman says that some Sufis even practice it wordlessly, knowing that no words can adequately express the language of the heart and soul. If you wish to learn more about this powerful prayer, read *The Illuminated Prayer* by Coleman Barks and Michael Green (Ballantine, 2000).

8
Questing

Who am I? Why am I here?

Most of us left such Big Questions behind when we left college and the late-night debates over warm Chianti about the Meaning of Life. Chances are that was a while ago. You now may have more years behind you than years left. You have a history of a "self" and that self's record of hopes, fears, dreams, and beliefs.

Stripped by trauma of our old certainties about life and self, we have the opportunity to dream new dreams for our lives, to hit an inner Reset button that allows for new possibilities. "It may be that when we no longer know what to do we have come to our real work," says poet Wendell Berry, "and that when we no longer know which way to go we have begun our real journey."

Years ago I spent many cold and rainy afternoons inside the warmth of the Seattle Aquarium. One of my favorite tanks was the home of several decorator crabs. I loved watching these crabs scuttle across the sandy floor fastening seaweed and bits of detritus to their shells to camouflage themselves from danger. They mirrored for me how we camouflage ourselves in Somebody Training: Take a piece of this belief from childhood religion, add a little bit of our parents' dreams for our lives and some cultural dictates about how we "ought" to be, and *voila!*, we are just like those decorator crabs, so crusted over that our Original Self is totally hidden.

Trauma is like some great tidal wave that rips through the tank of our lives, tearing away our carefully constructed camouflage. Minus the detritus of our former lives, we have a rare creative opportunity to ask Big Questions with an unencrusted heart. David Spangler holds that there are two broad categories of creativity. The first—with which we are most familiar—comes from reshaping what we already know. The second type of creativity arises in Wilderness, "Where we're not listening to the voices we've always listened to. We no longer have access to ways of thinking and perceiving that are familiar, that sustained and defined us. From this open space, something new can arise that is not just a reformulation of something we already know or have done.

"If we can embrace this open space and make it our ally, out of it will come new perceptions, new images, new awarenesses that will help us grow and prosper in ways that our old patterns couldn't. We have to ask, 'Who am I now? What am I to do and how am I to do it?'" David chuckled as he thought for a moment about how these questions had rearranged his own life. "Not easy questions. But very creative ones."

After my marriage ended, I felt as if I had hit a brick wall on the path of my life. I had always assumed I would get married, stay married with a happy family, make monthly deposits into my IRAs, and comfortably retire. I had prided myself on being a good couples' therapist and received good press about being a model premarriage counselor. Now here I was divorced and in such shaky financial shape that I had to debate about splurging for a latte.

All my assumptions about who I really was and where I was going went up in flames. All of the old answers to any questions I asked myself felt hollow, outworn, useless. I felt that I had returned to zero, with very little idea of who I was and where I was going.

Rabbi Zalman Schachter-Shalomi, a scholar of the Talmud, teaches that "In *the* Beginning. . ."—the words describing Creation that open the Old Testament—should really be translated, "In *a* Beginning." The Void precedes any beginning, not just the beginning of Creation; it is a primal state of pure potential which is the true prerequisite for any authentic new beginning. The more deeply we can allow ourselves to be emptied out, the more space, or void, is created for the gestation of a new life.

The Beginning, the Creation, will manifest at the *end* of your initiation. Right now, you are pregnant with that beginning, even though you may not feel that way. New Life may not be kicking yet, but it is there nonetheless. Your "pregnancy" is similar to the first trimester, when often the only way you know that you're pregnant is that you feel miserable.

The way we can most fully participate in this gestation period is to ask Big Questions without demanding immediate answers, and to dream new dreams, both asleep and awake.

ASKING BIG QUESTIONS

"In order to heal," sixteenth-century physician Gerhard Dorn once wrote, "one must learn to whom one belongs and to what end one has been created."

Asking Big Questions initiates a sacred quest for healing. Both "quest" and "question" issue from the same Latin root, *quaerare*, "to seek." As the hero or heroine in your own initiatory journey, you are seeking new life. You dwell in David Spangler's "still and open space," the Beginner's Mind of Zen Buddhism. This Beginner's Mind is considered holy space: "If your mind is empty, it is always ready for anything; it is open to everything," writes Buddhist teacher Suzuki Roshi in *Zen Mind, Beginner's Mind*. "In the beginner's mind there are many possibilities; in the expert's mind there are few." This open space is foundational to all spiritual quests. "Accustom your tongue to say, 'I do not know,'" advises the Talmud. "In order to arrive at a place you do not know," wrote the Christian mystic St. John of the Cross, "you must go by a way you do not know."

This reverence for Beginner's Mind stands in stark contrast to secular culture. Just try to remember a time when you were rewarded for responding, "I don't know," to a question posed you by parent, teacher, or boss. We learned very early on that for every question posed, there was an answer, and we had better know it. Throughout our school career we were graded on how well we could parrot back safe and predigested answers.

Wilderness returns us to Beginner's Mind. From this space of not-knowing, pregnant with possibility, we can ask open-ended questions free from familial or societal retribution. Here are questions we may not have allowed ourselves to ask for decades, perhaps even for a lifetime: Who am I, really? Why am I here? Whom do I truly love? In whom, or what, is my ultimate trust? Where do I find meaning in my life? (For other Big Questions, please see the Interlude at the end of this chapter.)

These Big Questions are not linear. You are not being given one line on an exam page to answer them.

Big Questions may have several answers, not one. The answers to Big Questions may not even be verbal: They might be feelings, intuitions, images. We may receive answers in the numinous symbols of dreams, the radical glory of a sunset, a lover's caress, a line of poetry, or a snatch of song. Answers may brazenly trumpet forth, or slip in as a barely audible internal whisper. The answer may actually be a deeper question. You might receive an answer as soon as you posit a question, but more often, the answer—or answers—may take days, weeks, months, or even years to arise to awareness.

The answers will come in their own time, in their own manner, bringing with them a deeper wisdom than our everyday minds can offer. What is most important is not that we grasp for answers, but that we love, and live into, the questions.

Darlene Cohen, a Buddhist who suffers from rheumatoid arthritis, suggests approaching Big Questions as modern versions of Zen koans, which are questions used to dislodge habituated thinking and open the self to a more spacious wisdom. Traditional koans were impossible to answer with the logical everyday mind (What is the sound of one hand clapping? Show me your face before you were born!). Koans carry tremendous power to break through conditioned reality into new ways of perceiving life, the world, and oneself.

"When we ask a question as a koan," writes Cohen in *Finding a Joyful Life in the Heart of Pain*, "we set in motion a powerful process that has the power to change the way we perceive everything. . . . We widen our screen in a curious, exploratory way, not necessarily looking for answers or immediate results. . . . What seems crucial to me is the proper framing and reframing of a question so that it excites curiosity and invites nonjudgmental exploration."

Nonjudgment is essential. We ask Big Questions in the spirit of play, curious to see what emerges. If we use the questions—or the answers we receive—as sticks with which to beat ourselves, we only create mental confusion, self-hatred, and emotional contraction.

As you explore, steer clear of nonhelpful questions, which often start with the word "why": "Why me? Why did I get this cancer? Why did my wife leave me? Why did the fire destroy everything I loved?" "Why" questions invite our rational minds to tromp wantonly over the tender ground of our hearts in search of The Answer. Remember, when we experience trauma we are initiated, willingly or no, into the Mysteries. Mysteries never yield The Answer; we will probably never know "why" something happened.

Jeanne Achterberg, a pioneer in the medical uses of guided imagery and a survivor of several traumas, including ocular melanoma and a devastating divorce, has her own special Big Question: "What contract have I made with life?" When she asks herself this after trauma, she remembers that "Life is meaningful, I do have a purpose, and I have some free will in establishing and renegotiating a life contract." Jeanne's Big Question reminds her that "My contract is to live a life full of human experience, a rich existence from which I could learn and ultimately teach. There is a Sufi saying that 'In order to know the Great One, you must learn to dance in both directions.' This sustains me—not fully, but mostly—during the most difficult and stressful circumstances." During initiation she revisits this contract, moves into the bigger space that the question invites, and makes the conscious choice to "renew" her contract with life at a deeper level.

VISIONING

"Sometimes I go about pitying myself, and all along my soul is being blown by great winds across the sky," goes an Ojibway saying. Sometimes we get so focused on just getting by after trauma that we fail to raise our vision, so to speak, and see that there is a greater process unfolding, that we as initiates are indeed being blown by the great winds of Spirit across the sky of our lives.

Questing for a vision is an integral part of most tribal rites of passage. Adolescents are sent into the wilderness to sit and fast until a vision comes, or sent on extensive walkabouts to discover their life purpose. Shamans in training are sent out in the same way to seek a vision for their lives.

We no longer live in tribal communities that support such visioning, but we can give such an experience to ourselves. "The most tragic failure of all is the failure to recognize our truest self, to hear its voice, and to allow it to guide us where we are meant to go. How easily we forget the spark the burns within us, urging us to become what we are capable of becoming!" declares Jungian analyst June Singer.

Sometimes that spark has been long buried under the ashes of everyday life. It was this way with Gretchen Schodde. As a young woman on a train ride to her grandfather's birthplace high in the Alps, sleepless with excitement, she had a vision of the purpose of her life: to be part of the creation of "a wellness community." Once home, though, her vision quickly faded amid the intense pressures of being a pioneering academic nurse-practitioner, negotiating the political rapids of a prestigious university position. Fifteen years after that train ride, her life broke down. Seriously ill from pneumonia that wouldn't resolve, on the edge of an emotional breakdown, Gretchen sought refuge at a women's retreat when she realized that her life was literally killing her. She left her academic career to spend a year gardening at the retreat center, completely releasing all ties to her old life.

Gretchen realized that being close to the earth was essential for her well-being. Tending the garden and cooking meals for retreatants allowed the time and space for her old dream to reemerge. After a year of prayer, silence, and surrender, she approached the manager of the vacant property next door and asked if she could caretake its main house. She called it "Harmony Hill," and her dream of creating a retreat center was born.

Sometimes that "spark that burns within us" ignites the fire of an entirely new dream and takes us in an entirely new direction.

Remember Anita, the marketing executive who walked away from friends into a surprising solitude? Although Anita had her "time-out," just as Gretchen did, she had never nourished a dream for her life. "I didn't know I could," she admits. "I always just did the next thing that I was good at. I never thought about what I wanted to do. It just seems like I ended up on this fast track that ate up my life but had enough rewards that I didn't want to question it too closely." Anita began asking herself the Big Questions during

Wilderness, and was met with silence for months. "It was so frustrating at first, like a muscle I had never used, asking those questions. I could only do it for a short amount of time without actually feeling woozy." Anita learned to meditate and slow down, and became more comfortable with inner silence.

Anita spent several years being willing to "not know" about the direction of her life. "Since I didn't have a clue what I wanted to do next, I put on a detective hat, asking myself what had given my life meaning. I began to see that I really loved helping people get where they wanted to go. My marketing company had been like that, only I wasn't willing to look too deeply at what I was actually helping people to sell."

Anita finally realized that she could put her marketing skills to good use working with nonprofit organizations whose work she believed in. "Everyone just wanted me to get over what happened fast, and get on with my life. If I hadn't given myself the time to grieve and the patience to incubate a new life, I would have done just that and been no better off for the experience, only a little more cynical and hard-edged. Instead, the terrible mess opened up a whole new life for me. I'm not as rich financially, but I'm a lot richer in every other way. I never would have asked for that much pain and loss, and would still never ask for it. But what I received, sticking with the process, was more magical than anything I could ever have conceived for my life."

How might you fan your own divine spark into a flame?

Begin with intention. Very credible scientific studies have proven the organizing and creative power of intention, something indigenous tribes have always known. When I worked with Puni, the Hawaiian huna I spoke of earlier, I asked him once to name the three most important spiritual principles I had to learn. He responded, "Intention, intention, and intention." Having clear intention organizes your life in ways we don't yet completely understand, setting up a powerful internal magnet that draws in new information and experiences. Make an intention, in your own words, for guidance for a new vision—professional, personal, spiritual, or all of the above—for your life. Post your intention on your computer desktop, your refrigerator, your bathroom mirror. Draw it, sing it, dance it, pray it.

Become more aware of synchronicities, or meaningful coincidences.
"Enter each day," advises Sam Keen, author of *A Passionate Life*, "with the expectation that the happenings of the day may contain a clandestine message addressed to you personally. Expect omens, epiphanies, casual blessings, and teachers who unknowingly speak to your condition." Invite life to speak to you in this way, giving you additional guidance for the unfolding of your vision. (Synchronicity is often defined, tongue-in-cheek, as "God acting anonymously.") Make an intention for synchronicities to appear in your life that can point the way to a new future.

Ellen, a workshop participant, called me six months after a retreat to tell me about her experience of synchronicity. After making an intention for a new vision for her life, she began to doodle in the margins of her datebook. In the week after she started doodling, her mother made a chance remark about Ellen loving to draw as a child (something she had not remembered), and a friend invited her to an art opening. Finally, that same week, she got lost one free afternoon on the way to the grocery store and ended up in an unfamiliar area of town. Ellen asked for inner guidance on where to go, turned left, and ended up in front of an art store. She suddenly put together all four occurrences and then spent several hours exploring all the media in the art store, even signing up for a watercolor class. Watercolor turned into a hobby, which grew into a passion, which developed several years later into a new career. When an out-of-the-ordinary event or combination of events—no matter how small—catches your attention, ask yourself "What might this mean to me?" Then play with the possible answers.

Look back on your life. Sometimes, understanding our past better can prepare us for a new future. William Bridges, author of *Transitions*, counsels those in Wilderness to write an autobiography. "Sometimes it is only in seeing where you have been," writes Bridges, "that you can tell where you are headed." Reflect on themes in your life; discover your high points and nadirs. Try writing your autobiography in five pages or less, and then read it as if it were a stranger's. Ask yourself: What sort of person is this? What needs resolution? What is asking to emerge? What has this person been seeking without knowing it? How did mistakes become teachers, and difficulties emerge as gifts?

How many times have you said to yourself, "If only I could...?" In Wilderness, whatever has held us back—a person, a belief, a set of circumstances—has often vanished. What haven't you done that you'd love to try? Live out of your imagination instead of your history: Treat yourself to doing what gives you joy, even if it seems silly or at right angles to the rest of your life. I loved to dance as a child, but whatever dancing career I might have had was squashed when my third-grade ballet teacher sarcastically introduced me to the recital audience as her "finest" student. I wanted the floor to open up and swallow me. It didn't, but I never took dance lessons again. After my divorce, I realized I had been wistfully telling myself, "If only I could take a dance class" for years, but had always come up with "reasonable" excuses: the shape of my body, money, time. I finally signed up for a beginner's adult modern dance class, and my spirit learned how to take flight in joy during some very challenging times. The metaphor of dancing became my touchstone for post-divorce recovery and remains one of my primary life metaphors to this day.

Opening to our heart's desire may feel daunting after a lifetime of "desire override." Start with small steps. Like Anita's, our "vision muscle" may be seriously atrophied. We may need to strengthen it by taking small steps before taking on anything big like "my career" or "the rest of my life."

Cynthia didn't have a clue what she wanted for her life after she began to recover from her rape. I suggested to her that she cast about her everyday life and look for something she wanted to change. With new eyes, Cynthia realized with a shock that she had always slept in whatever sheets she had been able to find at a secondhand store. She decided to take herself to a department store to buy new sheets and a bedspread. To her chagrin, it took her the better part of a day. Overwhelmed by all the choices of color, unsure of herself, she needed to periodically return to her car and just sit. She returned home, changed her bed, and found that her life changed, too, in a small way. She came back to her next session with me with a grin that stayed on for almost the whole time. With the confidence and courage gained from what she had first criticized as a "stupid, small thing," Cynthia was able to take other small, playful steps toward a new life that better fit her heart and soul.

With this visioning process in Wilderness, play with small steps, not huge leaps. "Play" is the key word here: play with new activities, identities, outings. People in Wilderness commonly play with new haircuts, different clothing, fresh routes to work. However, this is usually not the time to make big decisions and big changes; clarity about these will emerge later. Now is the time to play with small choices, relishing the new creativity that comes with playing with new elements in new ways.

BIG DREAMS

Every night when you drop into sleep, your "inner elder" has your undivided attention. That deeper, wiser part of you—by whatever name you choose to call it—may speak more clearly during initiation than at any other time in your life. Vivid dreams and nightmares are common during initiation. Research shows that the number and intensity of dreams increase during life crises. During and after those crises, we begin to dream earlier in our sleep cycles, and the dreams trigger more powerful brain activity than the dreams we have at other times in our lives.

The dream itself can help initiate a dreamer into a deeper level of consciousness, says Emma Bezy, M.S.W., Director of the Center for Spirit & Health. "In this culture when we have so few overt initiatory processes, there's a way that dreams serve as a substitute," says Bezy. "If I can't actually go out into the wilderness to receive a vision from Spirit on a vision quest, I can get a microcosmic version of that through dreamtime. The dream can be our ally in this way during Wilderness."

Indeed, in traditional cultures dreams were seen as a way for the Sacred to break through into human consciousness. We can allow ourselves to be instructed by the nocturnal visitations of that inner elder. Dreams during Wilderness—and beyond into Rebirth—can be Big Dreams, showing us our next steps in healing, highlighting unrecognized feelings and unmet needs, stimulating insights, and enhancing our ability to work with the powerful forces of transformation.

Louise Mahdi, a Jungian analyst who leads adolescents and adults on vision quests and wilderness rites of passage, is fond of calling Big Dreams "endangered species." She has found them, though, to be common during Wilderness. "An ordinary dream," says Mahdi, "is like a little flashlight that can guide you through a night or two. A Big Dream is like the beacon of a lighthouse, shining out far over the waters so that one can see for some distance, over the next several months or years or even the next chapter of one's life. These Big Dreams offer new images and possibilities for one's life to be lived in a very new way."

What makes a Big Dream big? When you have one, you'll know it. They are very different than regular dreams: more intensity of color, acuity of sound, touch, taste. We awake with the sense of having trod on holy ground, of having glimpsed some reality that is bigger and brighter than our waking one. Big dreams are transformational in the deepest sense; if worked with and honored, they have the capacity to change and guide our life, not over a short time like "regular" dreams, but over months, years, or even a lifetime. These Big Dreams are not to be analyzed or dissected like ordinary dreams but are meant to be lived into, just like Big Questions.

When I was seriously ill with chronic fatigue syndrome, I was in a hurry to get on with my life. I investigated anything that held hope for a cure, but nothing worked. I was very frustrated, in a serious hurry; I wanted to be done with this healing business and get on with things.

Then one night I had this Big Dream:

I am in a hurry to get to Phoenix. I speed up the entrance ramp to the express lane to Phoenix, only to find myself turned back by workmen who inform me I can't go this way. I then drive up the regular ramp to the highway, only again to be turned back. In desperation, I get out of the car and look around the desert for an alternate route. I see an abandoned bicycle, which I throw myself on and begin to pedal madly in the right direction. I am stopped abruptly by an old man, who tells me I must go to Phoenix on foot. I am very angry at him, throw the bicycle down, and begin walking. He stops me again, unperturbed by my frustration, and says, "No, you must go barefoot. You must really see the ground you travel." I give up, sigh, and take off my shoes. I guess there's no other way to Phoenix. I remove my shoes and am surprised at the wonderful feel of the red desert dust beneath my feet. The old man smiles, and points toward Phoenix, now giving me permission to go.

I look down at the desert I'm traveling, and am astonished to find, instead of a lifeless tract of sand, beautiful gems lying everywhere, half-buried in the dirt.

I woke from this dream astonished at its clarity. I had been in a rush to get to Phoenix (the bird of transformation that rises reborn from its old ashes), as I have always been in a rush to be in the future. The dream informed me that the path *was* the journey, that *how* I got to Phoenix was the point. I drew the old man's image that week, and returned to him often in the ensuing months. I gave myself permission to notice what half-buried "gems" were already in my life, in a time and place that I had considered useless and lifeless. Twenty years later, I still return to the power of that dream when I find myself so focused on the "destination" that I have forgotten about the journey itself.

Big Dreams can be about meeting powerful animals as guides, finding treasures in unexpected places, journeying to new lands, or encountering spiritual beings or tutelary animals. We are meant to respond to these dreams, not analyze them. Jungian analyst James Hillman stresses keeping the dream symbols alive rather than reducing them to one-liners. In response to the dream image of a black dog that one of his clients had, he advised: "It is better to keep the dream's black dog before your inner sense all day than to 'know' its meaning (sexual impulses, mother complex, devilish aggression, guardian, or what have you). A living dog is better than one stuffed with concepts or substituted by an interpretation."

We can use Active Imagination to go back, as I did, and learn more from those who appear in our dreams. We can simply go back to the dream and reexperience it in all its numinous power. We can draw the dream, or part of the dream, not as a way of making art, but as a way of bringing the gift of the dream more deeply into waking reality. We can dance the dream, sculpt the dream, enact the dream by ourselves or with others. We can ask, "What does this dream want of me? How might I live my life differently in response to this ?"

The Navajo believe that dreams can sometimes prescribe specific curing rituals. While we don't have curing rituals in our culture, we can turn a Big Dream into one. A client had a terrifying Big Dream about a large snake coming up through a deep fissure in the floor of his living room and demanding his attention, blocking any exit from the room as he ran from door to door.

The more he resisted, the larger it grew, until it wrapped around his neck and began suffocating him. Jason had always disliked snakes. I encouraged him to read up on them as symbols, and he discovered that they represent many things: our ability to "shed" old lives, the wisdom that comes up from the depths of Mystery (as his snake rose up from that dark fissure), and ultimately healing, as in the two intertwined snakes on the caduceus of physicians.

Jason realized he was resisting a deeper level of shedding that he needed to do, and that he needed to learn to trust the wisdom and healing that arise from darkness. With this intention, he began to visit the reptile house at the zoo, and as his distaste lessened, he visited a local pet store where they allowed him to handle several snakes. He finally bought a small snake, which withdrew into a small ceramic "cave" the week after he bought it. Concerned, he returned to the pet store to get some advice. Jason learned that, synchronistically, the snake was shedding its skin! The pet store owner informed him that it was uncomfortable for the snake; it might not eat or drink for a while. The owner also told him that shedding a skin was hard work, and the snake was quite vulnerable while shedding, hence the necessity to disappear into a cave.

Jason was able to apply the same lessons metaphorically to himself. It gave him permission to withdraw from the world and go inside of himself, which he had been resisting, and to simply allow the discomfort of this time, which he had been denying by working overtime at the office. Jason learned to sit with his snake, each in his own "cave," and when the snake emerged with fresh new skin, Jason took the old skin and put it on a small altar he had on his bedroom window sill, to remind himself that he was undergoing the same process, and new wisdom, and new life, would soon emerge.

We are blessed with a rich and exuberant sort of creativity during Wilderness. In this creativity, loosed from the restrictive moorings of business-as-usual, we can seek new visions for our life, ask Big Questions, dream new dreams. Ancient heroes quested after treasure buried in caves. As contemporary heroes and heroines, we quest after the priceless treasure of our hopes and dreams, which has been long buried in the recesses of our own hearts and souls.

Interlude Eight

JOURNAL: BIG QUESTIONS

Go through this list of Big Questions. Which ones engage you? Excite you? Scare you? Irritate you? Select a question and write it in your journal. Feel free to reword in your own language. If another Big Question announces itself, one that invites you to open-hearted exploration, write it down, too.

- Who am I, really?
- Why am I here?
- Whom do I truly love? By whom am I truly loved?
- In whom, or what, is my ultimate trust?
- What would be unlived or undone (talents, dreams, relationships, ideas) in my life if it ended today?
- Where do I find meaning in my life? How may I create a life that allows for more of this?
- How have I harmed myself or others? How may I make amends?
- What is my relationship to my Creator? What needs updating or release in my spiritual life?
- What stands in the way of my allowing my life to be guided by Spirit?
- What do I yearn for? What is my heart's desire?
- What have I always dreamed of doing? Why haven't I done it?
- What are my top priorities and values? Do I actually live by those priorities, or simply give them lip service?
- What am I most afraid of? What do I need to do to release these fears?
- What have I contributed to life, to others, to myself?
- From what am I running away? What resources do I need to face it?

- What is (are) the most important thing(s) I can learn from this trauma and this initiation?

Here's another important Big Question, one that we rarely ask ourselves: What feeds my soul? We think of famine and starvation only in terms of swollen bellies and sunken cheeks, but we are a nation of soul-starved people. Our refrigerators are full, but our spirits are often empty. Meditating on this Big Question can save your soul, and transform your life.

Give yourself some uninterrupted time. If you wish, play some favorite music quietly in the background and light a candle, asking for guidance and support. Breathe into the question, and then simply start writing. Allow yourself to write *around* the question: What does your body feel in response to the question? Your heart? What memories are triggered? What images? (Draw the images in your journal, if you like.) What hopes and dreams? What griefs and fears? When you've written everything you can with your dominant hand, switch to your nondominant hand. Give your nondominant hand permission to respond in new ways. If you wish, ask your inner Wisdom Guide to respond to the question as well, through your nondominant hand.

Honor the question as a koan. Let it sink into your heart of hearts and rest there undisturbed. See what emerges. Ask for a dream. Put on some favorite music: Dance the question and your body's response. In meditation, ask for an image, draw it, and place it on your altar. Take the question for a walk (see below). Trust non-knowing. The deepest answers will emerge in their own time.

DREAM JOURNAL

Wilderness is a time to reorient your internal antenna in the direction of your dreams. Choosing to pay attention to them will increase your ability to receive them and your capacity to remember and work with them for guidance.

You can increase your chances of having a Big Dream by saying a prayer before sleep for a dream, or making an intention for the same. I made a small clay "dream bowl," which I now keep beside my bed. When I need a dream for guidance or a healing dream, I write my prayer for such on a small piece of paper and place it in the bowl.

Try to give yourself time in the morning to remember your dreams before you spring (or stumble!) from bed. If you can manage to stay in the same position you woke in, your dream recall will be enhanced.

Keep your initiation journal by your bed to record your dreams. You may also want to keep a small flashlight by the bed to record middle-of-the-night dreams. (When I do this, I write them on a separate piece of paper, given their near-illegibility, and later transcribe them into my journal.) The meaning of many dreams, particularly Big Dreams, will be immediately obvious; others will take time and some effort on your part to understand. For several different ways of working with dreams, see the Resources at the end of this book.

You can honor any symbols or images that arise from Big Dreams by drawing them, sculpting them, or writing a word or two about their essence or the message of the dream itself. Place them on your altar with an intention to learn more from them, or allow them to guide your life, and light a candle or tea light. When I had the Big Dream about going to Phoenix, I filled a tiny dish with red sand, and half-buried several small pieces of polished red jasper in it. I sat in front of my altar and meditated on the dish, or actually ran my fingers through the sand and felt the smooth coolness of the jewels buried there. That tangible representation of my Big Dream gave me courage and hope during some dark times.

VISION WALK

Tribal cultures send initiates out on vision quests where it is assumed that Spirit will send coded messages through the natural world for the initiate to decipher. The vision quester seeks meaning in everything that happens, from the circling of a hawk to an unexpected wind springing up during prayers.

Most of us lack the inner calling to undergo the rigors of a full vision quest. But most of us are capable of taking a vision walk. Pick a walk or a hike where you can walk undisturbed for at least an hour. Set an intention for the walk. This intention can be any one of the Big Questions; it could also be an answer to another question you have about your life or its direction. You may also simply ask for guidance in the largest sense; sometimes I just pray, "Speak to me!" Before you begin, breathe out and release anything besides your intention that is cluttering your mind, say a prayer for guidance if you wish, and begin your walk. Practice "soft vision": Rather than looking hard for "signs," allow yourself to receive what is happening around you. Be open for anything that catches your attention, from a crumpled soda can at your feet to the way the light catches the leaves in the trees above you. Walk from a place of curiosity and receptivity.

When I was writing Chapter Eight, I felt increasingly bogged down mentally. I decided it was time to take a vision walk about this book. I set off up the path from Harmony Hill into the mountains, after praying for guidance about my writing fatigue. I was so tired that I looked down at each step as I walked. I heard a whooshing sound about me and looked up just in time to see a hawk flying ten feet above my head. It got my attention. I watched the hawk circle around me three times, and then take off for parts unknown. I asked myself what that hawk might be telling me about my question, and I understood immediately: Wake up, get your head out of the details, and remember the Big Picture! I was able to return to my writing refreshed and renewed.

Any event, or any object, can have deep meaning on a vision walk. If you're unsure about what a sign means, lightly ask yourself, "If I *did* know what this sign meant, what might it be?" Some signs are immediately apparent; others may take a while to decipher. Play with meaning; you'll know when you've "got it" when you get goosebumps or tingling, a feeling of rightness or lightness, or a calm "knowing." Record your insights in your journal.

Another way to take a vision walk is by walking the labyrinth, one of the oldest transformational tools known to humankind. A labyrinth—as opposed to a maze, with its confusing choices of paths—has only one path to the center. Walking this path can represent the journey of your initiation, or a quest for the answer to a Big Question. You may find a labyrinth near you by using the Internet Labyrinth Locator at www.gracecathedral.org/labyrinth, or by looking at the resources in my book *Exploring the Labyrinth: A Guide to Healing and Spiritual Growth*.

Before you enter the labyrinth, pause. Be clear about your intention for the walk. As I explain in my book, you can have the same sort of intentions as for a vision walk, or you can simply walk in, as I'm fond of saying, "empty-handed and open-hearted," open for guidance as it unfolds. Bring your journal if you wish; the center of the labyrinth is an excellent place to stop and write, pray, and be receptive to guidance. The labyrinth can be a powerful place of inspiration, guidance, and support for you, as it has been for thousands of other journeyers.

9
Gratitude and Grace

When you're in the midst of recovery from trauma, probably the last thing on your mind is thoughts of gratitude. In fact, if someone were to say that you should feel grateful in some way for the experience, you might feel angry. In the early stages of recovery, even to mention grace and gratitude seems like a harsh mockery of the pain. But now that you are reaching the end of Wilderness, it is time to explore these gifts, both as harbingers of New Life and as catalysts for it as well. Gratitude is a gift we can give ourselves; grace is a free gift from Spirit.

Gratitude was certainly not what my client Cynthia expected to experience nine months after her rape and assault. She was sitting on the couch in my therapy office, legs tucked under her, with a bemused expression on her face. "Yesterday morning, I was drinking my coffee before heading off to work. I'd had a hard night with some nightmares, not much sleep. I tried to meditate, but I was too tired, so I just sat looking out the window. I was watching a robin eat holly berries, feeling pretty lousy, when all of a sudden I realized what an incredible thing it was to be alive, even in my condition," Cynthia recalled.

When I asked her to tell me more, she responded, "Well, I thought, 'How weird to feel this way,' but my heart felt like singing just like that robin. It didn't make the earth shake, but it was like the sun breaking through some pretty heavy clouds. I started to think about everything I had to be grateful for: supportive friends, a job that paid the bills, a body that I'm beginning to trust again and that can take me running, a roof over my head. But a small, tight part of me interrupted and said, 'You know, Cynthia, this isn't reasonable. You got raped, remember?' And then a larger part of me replied, 'Yeah, I know. This isn't about pretending that didn't happen, or denying how awful I've felt. It's about seeing that life continues, and even in the middle of something so awful, there's a whole lot to be grateful for.'"

One day your internal tides begin to turn. Your life eases up ever so slightly; recovering from your trauma doesn't consume you as it has. Cynthia awoke one morning to experience grace in the angle of the morning sunlight, in the way the robin cocked his head, in the crimson of the holly berries against the dark green glossiness of the leaves. Grace opened her heart (or, perhaps, her heart opened to allow grace in), and in response she became aware of all there was to be thankful for.

Grace and gratitude both issue from the same Latin root, *gratias*. From this Latin root come the many expressions for "thank you": *gracias* in Spanish, *grazie* in Italian. We have the custom of saying grace over meals in thanks for the gift of the food. Grace and gratitude are inextricably intertwined. Hospice chaplain Kathleen Dowling Singh says that just as grace and gratitude come from the same linguistic source, the qualities of grace and gratitude have their origin in the same spiritual source.

FINDING GRATITUDE

When I was feeling lacerated and betrayed during early recovery from memories of childhood sexual abuse, I couldn't, and didn't, find much cause for gratitude. What was there to be grateful for when my world had collapsed?

Then one day in a bookstore *Simple Abundance*, a book by Sarah Ban Breathnach, nearly jumped off the shelf at me. I bought it and curled up with it in bed that night. She wrote eloquently about gratitude in a way that didn't seem Pollyanna-ish, and suggested bedtime as a time to consciously count our blessings. I thought, "Why not? I've got nothing left to lose." I got out my journal and decided to make a list of what I was grateful for.

It was a very slow start. Part of me didn't want to look for anything to be grateful for, as if finding gratitude would somehow discount the reality of my suffering. Writing in my journal that first night was, more than anything else, an act of will. I started, literally, very close to home: irises blooming in a cobalt vase beside me; a warm, comfortable bed; my small daughter sleeping peacefully in the next room.

The next evening proved a little easier. I looked further afield and found gratitude for wonderful friends, the blue and green lushness of Puget Sound, my women's circle which had been meeting for a decade. As time wore on, I began to feel as if I were spinning my own version of *The Arabian Nights*, the Persian story in which the heroine stretched and embellished a story to last 1,001 nights, ending with a cliff-hanger each night to entice her sultan back for more. I became curious about what would show up on my gratitude page, even as my old world and self were crumbling to pieces.

After the first several weeks, something wonderful happened: I began to carry "gratitude awareness" into my daytime life. As I ran out of the obvious gratitudes, I had to look for smaller gratitudes that I could later record in my journal: the postman's cheerful hello, the crisp first bite of a freshly picked apple, even the momentary satisfaction of a clean kitchen. My eyes started reopening to the small everyday delights I had been running roughshod over in my hurry to "get on" with life.

I must admit that this process didn't magically change my life. It didn't mitigate the trauma. What it did do, though, was transform my relationship to my pain. I learned to be grateful in the midst of a time of deep suffering. Learning to consciously practice gratitude under these circumstances helped keep my heart open at a time when I wanted to close it and keep it permanently shuttered against further wounding. The conscious practice of gratitude kept my heart soft at a low ebb in my trust of life.

Vipassana teacher Philip Moffit writes in *Yoga Journal*:

> *Practicing mindfulness of gratitude consistently leads to a direct experience of being connected to life and the realization that there is a larger context in which your personal story is unfolding. Cultivating thankfulness for*

being part of life blossoms into a feeling of being blessed, not in the sense of winning the lottery, but in a more refined appreciation for the interdependent nature of life. It also elicits feelings of generosity, which create further joy. Gratitude can soften a heart that has become too guarded, and it builds the capacity for forgiveness, which creates the clarity of mind that is ideal for spiritual development.

PRACTICING GRATITUDE

It's easy to feel grateful when life is great. It's a whole lot more challenging when our lives have been slammed by trauma. When life is hard, the practice of gratitude becomes a spiritual practice, a conscious choice to open our hearts at a time when our hearts are most likely to be closed.

Just as we meditate whether we feel like it or not, gratitude becomes life-bestowing when we practice it whether or not we feel in the mood. Most of the world's great religions consider thankfulness in all circumstances to be a spiritual decision, a marker of how we relate to the gift of life itself. "A thankful person is thankful under all circumstances," wrote Bahaullah, the founder of the Baha'i faith: "A complaining soul complains even if he lives in Paradise." Fourteenth-century Christian mystic Meister Eckhart said, "If the only prayer you say in your whole life is 'thank you,' that would suffice." Rabbi Abraham Joshua Heschel says, "It is gratefulness that makes the soul great."

Gratitude is not a denial of difficulties; it is not about being sentimental or seeing the world through rose-colored glasses. We can practice gratitude when we're feeling awful, when our heart is tight and shuttered. Gratitude won't change the outer events in our lives, but it will change our relationship to, and our experience of, them.

Living in an affluent and greedy culture, we take so much for granted. In our rush to get ahead, we shutter our vision to the important basic things: a roof over our head, a loving family or group of friends, food on the table. Add to that culture-sickness the pain of trauma, when we are most likely to see life through a dark filter, and we end up with tremendous suffering. Consciously practicing gratitude removes that dark filter, and brings to the foreground all the riches of the life we live, even in the midst of pain.

What is there to be thankful for when your world is in shambles? Here are some possibilities:

- Breath. Each breath is a gift of life itself, an infusion of Spirit (the words for "breath" and "spirit" are the same in many cultures around the world and through time).
- Body parts that work and keep working no matter how we are feeling emotionally: eyes, ears, fingers. A powerful gratitude exercise, particularly if you are challenged with illness, is to go through your body, part by part, and give thanks for everything that does work.
- People who love and support you
- Animals who love and support you
- The food on your table at each meal represents a long line of those who have served. For a grace at mealtime, try thanking each person who has had anything to do with your food: grocery clerks and checkout people, delivery people who got it to the store, people who harvested it, the farmers who grew it. Then thank all the plants and animals who have given their essence to nourish you. Finally, thank all the elements that helped your food to grow: sun, wind, rain, soil, microorganisms. An extraordinary amount of time and effort went into making the food now sitting before you.
- A roof over your head
- A comfortable bed
- A good meal shared with friends
- Sunrises and sunsets
- The beauty of nature, such as spring flowers or fall leaves

Remember to include yourself in your gratitudes. A friend pointed this out to me after I had been writing my gratitudes for several months. I went back into my journal and saw that I had never expressed any gratitude for my own gifts or coping abilities in some very dark times. I consciously spent the next week writing only gratitudes for myself (including gratitude that I was willing to spend the time to be grateful for me), and emerged from that week feeling stronger, more resilient, and more deeply appreciative and trusting of myself.

FIERCE GRACE

The conscious practice of gratitude can open us to receiving grace. "Grace" is one of those slippery spiritual words that means lots of things to some people, and hardly anything, I think, to even more. I'll share with you my own definition: Grace is an always-available gift from Spirit, a state of consciousness that reconnects us with our own souls, with our Higher Power, with the heartbeat of life forever pulsating in and around us. "The winds of grace are always blowing," the Hindu saint Ramakrishna once said; "what we must do is learn to raise our sails."

Ram Dass, the teacher who blazed a spiritual trail for many, was stricken with a massive cerebral hemorrhage while writing a book on aging and given a ten-percent chance of survival. Partially paralyzed, confined to a wheelchair, his speech severely impaired, Ram Dass had to find his way back into life again. After railing against life and God, he pulled himself out of a deep depression and began to investigate how his new disabilities might be the next level for his spiritual and soul growth.

Ram Dass began to call his stroke "fierce grace" because it brought him into what he calls his "Soul level" through its ferocity. "When we are able to get to our souls, where we can see things as God sees them, we experience our lives as grace," Ram Dass said in an interview in *Parabola*. "We're looking at it all from a different perspective."

That "God's eye view," that fierce grace, enabled Ram Dass to return to life more deeply human, with new spiritual wisdom to teach and offer others. "We struggle against the inevitable, and we all suffer because of it," he writes in *Still Here: Embracing Aging, Changing, and Dying*. "We have to find another way to look at the whole process of being born, changing, and dying, some kind of perspective that might allow us to deal with what we perceive as big obstacles without having to be dragged through the drama." Even though he admits this fierce grace doesn't solve everything, "It really helps to understand that we have something—that we are something—which is unchangeable, beautiful, completely aware, and continues no matter what."

Trauma is that same fierce grace for us all. When we have been broken down, and broken open, by trauma, we lose our smaller, smugger, less conscious perspective on our own lives and on life itself. Initiation offers us the opportunity to embrace fierce grace, consciously raising our sails to the winds of spirit that can carry us into New Life. We can open to a new and very different consciousness, the truth of love and compassion.

Emma Bezy sees grace as "a gift, an inexplicable and surprising capacity to cope with, and grow though, a very difficult life circumstance. We don't think we have the resources and yet somehow some deeper, wiser part of us does move through it. We find we don't have to do it alone; Something out there and 'in here' that is bigger than me supports me in very surprising ways. This force of love doesn't care if I've behaved right or been a good human or eaten all my vegetables. It's totally independent of whether I 'deserve' it or not."

The whole concept of grace is one that has confused and challenged me throughout my life. Unlike Emma, I got caught in old theological constructs about trying to be good enough to deserve it. What I have learned over and over, though, it that it is not a matter of "deserving."

Everyone I've talked with about grace stresses the "gift" aspect. It appears at totally unexpected times. You can't "make" it happen. Cynthia experienced it watching the robin eat holly berries. Gretchen Schodde felt graced during her long months of chemotherapy whenever she received a prayerful and loving message from someone in her e-mail support group. Jason found grace in giving himself over to an unhurried afternoon of cooking a meal. Anita discovered that curling up with her cat on the couch opened her to grace. Samuel found that whenever he touched the mezuzah in the front hall of his house, he felt awakened to the presence of God working through grace in his life. I know that making the time for both meditation and prayer helps me raise my sails for the rest of the day

Once we discover what raises our sails, we can start consciously creating time for these activities. As Ramakrishna said, grace is like a big holy wind blowing all the time. We can never capture or bottle it, but we can learn to invoke grace both by raising our sails more frequently and by increasing the quality and size of our sails through practice and intention.

When grace "shows up," it fills our hearts; releases pain, fear, and anxiety; liberates us from the prison of isolation; and reconnects us with ourselves, with

God, and with life. Grace can never be grasped, held onto, or owned. It can, however, be received with gratitude, again and again.

Bo Lozoff, founder of the Ashram Prison Project and author of *It's a Meaningful Life: It Just Takes Practice*, enjoys telling his favorite story about grace. Lozoff once accompanied Rabbi Sholomo Carlebach on a speaking tour as his guitarist. One evening the Rabbi told his audience that "Full experiences of God can never be planned or achieved. They are spontaneous moments of grace." Lozoff felt confused, and later that night asked the Rabbi, "If God-realization is just accidental, why do we work so hard doing all these spiritual practices?" To which the Rabbi replied, "To be as accident-prone as possible!"

The process of initiation inclines you to be accident-prone. All of the practices in this book—surrender, gratitude, prayer, journal keeping—are designed to make you, as the Rabbi said, as accident-prone as possible. Poet Leonard Cohen writes:

> *Ring the bells that still can ring*
> *Forget your perfect offering*
> *There is a crack in everything*
> *That's how the light gets in.*

Allow the fierce grace of your initiatory journey to wake you up. Allow yourself to receive grace, to call upon its power, to practice gratitude, and know that the crack of your trauma is how the light of Spirit can enter and heal your life.

Interlude Nine

GRATITUDE FOR A NEEDED QUALITY

Denise Lin claims that if you allow yourself to become consciously grateful for something around you, you will begin to take on the qualities of whatever you are grateful for, and the qualities will take root and grow in you. "For instance," she suggests in *Quest*, "If you feel a deep, fulfilling gratitude for the old gnarled oak that has again and again survived the trials of time, you begin to imbue yourself with those same qualities of strength and endurance. Whatever qualities you focus your attention on, in the spirit of gratefulness, will begin to develop within you."

Play with this notion. What qualities do you most need to cultivate at this point in your initiatory journey? Patience? Trust? Love? Strength? When you know what they are, spend some detective time looking for something in your world that represents them: Your cat may embody staying in the present moment; the sky may represent expansiveness; a stand of bamboo swaying in the wind may speak to you about flexibility. When you find your "teacher," spend quiet time with it. Open your heart to your teacher in gratitude for the quality it expresses. As your heart opens, breathe in that quality from your teacher. Move back and forth between expressing gratitude for the quality in your teacher and allowing yourself to receive it. Imagine the quality filling you, body and soul. Let your cells drink it in. Allow yourself to fill to overflowing with it. If you wish, ask your teacher, in whatever way you wish, how you might embody and live that quality more deeply. Your teacher may respond with words, images, sensations, or nonverbal "knowing." When you are done, thank your "teacher" for teaching you about that quality.

CULTIVATING THANKFULNESS FOR EVERYTHING

Be aware that this one is a graduate-level gratitude exercise! By learning to find something to be grateful for in every experience of your life, you will cultivate a state of mind and heart that will begin to recognize the gifts of your initiatory journey. Don't try it if you're still struggling with trying to find reasons to be grateful in your everyday life. Wait to do this exercise until you're feeling a little bit stronger and more resilient.

Begin to review your life, noting in your journal all the rough spots, both the minor ones and the biggies. When you have a list, start with one of the minor ones. Take a deep breath, and ask for support and guidance in finding something to be grateful for in that experience. Write down three things you're grateful for, even if at first they seem a little far-fetched. For instance, you might find that you discovered an inner resilience that you had not known about before; you developed a deeper trust in the process of life, that when one door closes, another one always opens; you learned to open to the support and caring of friends to get you through. What did you learn or discover through the experience? What qualities did the situation invite you to cultivate, what hidden strengths or resources did you discover? How is your life larger or better as a result? (You may write more than three if you find more!)

Work your way up bit by bit, over time, to the larger hurts and traumas. You'll find that you slowly, over time, develop a spiritual muscle that can see the gifts in almost anything. Remember, this is not about being Pollyanna and glossing over suffering; it is about cultivating a larger vision that can hold your suffering in a healing context. This exercise can begin to transform the way you see your past, and in so doing, offer you strength, courage, and hope for both your initiatory journey and your future.

RAISING YOUR SAILS
Heart Breathing

Opening your heart is akin to raising the sails of your soul.

Give yourself ten to twenty minutes of undisturbed time. Settle into your favorite posture for meditation. Imagine you can breathe directly in and out of your heart, inhaling and exhaling through the middle of your chest. Allow your heart to soften and open throughout the process, releasing layer upon even deeper layer of armoring and protection. If you find your thoughts wandering, simply return your attention to breathing through your heart.

When your heart feels soft, spacious, and open, look around you, still continuing to breathe through your heart. Allow your eyes to become as soft as your heart; feel the connection between these soft eyes and your soft heart. How does the room look, smell, sound, and feel different?

Think about your own initiatory journey. From this perspective of the breathing heart, what do you notice now about your own journey? How do its pain and its suffering look from this perspective? What do you realize, and know, from this heart-breathing perspective that is more difficult to remember from the perspective of a tight, enclosed heart?

PART THREE: REBIRTH

10
New Life

THE COMING OF SPRING

No matter how gray and dreary your landscape looks now, it will begin to change as you move toward Rebirth. Some morning, you're going to wake up and things will be different. I don't necessarily mean hugely different: no earthshaking change, no light cascading down upon you, no special e-card announcing your New Life.

This difference will probably be tiny, so subtle you might miss it if you don't know where to look or if you're too distracted by the business of your everyday life to pay attention.

The best way I can describe this is to talk from my experience of living in the Pacific Northwest. Our winters are long—very, very long. Month upon month of daily rain, dusky light even at midday, constant cloud cover, and fourteen hours of darkness make for a long and often depressing season. Toward February, Northwesterners start wondering if the other seasons were just a figment of our stir-crazy imagination. Then, it always happens, every year. I'll be taking one of my forced walks in the rain around my neighborhood, and there's something different in the sodden air . . . a slight warmth, a feeble ray of sunshine breaking through the dense clouds, an intangible shiver of life to come. I'll start searching for these early signs of spring, and there it is one morning: a green tip breaking through the crusty winter mulch. The first crocus, or to be completely accurate, the first tiny green tip of the shoot.

If I didn't know to look for this sign of spring, I would miss it. Once I see it, though, I begin to notice lovely green promises of new life appearing everywhere.

When I start seeing green, I breathe differently. I hold myself differently. I know there's hope, even if I'm standing in a forty-degree drizzle. I know—although I don't know exactly when—that spring is around the corner.

After we go through Loss and Wilderness, the signs of Rebirth are the same way. William Bridges writes in *Transitions* that, although we long for the unmistakable, irrefutable "big sign" that Rebirth is coming, "We must settle for inner signals that alert us to the proximity of new beginnings. The most important of these signal begins as a faint intimation of something different, a new theme in the music, a strange fragrance on the breeze. Because the signal is subtle, it is hard to perceive when other stimuli are strong. This first hint may take the form of either an inner idea or of an external opportunity, buts its hallmark is not a logical sign of validity but a resonance that it sets up in us."

Just as we know when fall is in the air, or spring, we'll know when something about our life is different, subtle but different. The beginnings of Rebirth are the same. No drama, no voice speaking from the heavens, but a certain sense that the winds are changing. Spring is on the way, even if you look outside and see a sodden wintry mess.

No clear demarcation lies between Wilderness and Rebirth. There is no line to step over, not even a metaphorical one, as there was between Loss and Wilderness. When you feel that intimation of something different, that hint of new life on the breeze, know that Rebirth is around the corner.

In Chapter Five, you met Samuel, a successful businessman who had lost everything to bankruptcy. During a retreat, he had created a model of his Wilderness. The floor of his "forest" was made out of clay into which he had stuck nothing but dead, broken-off twigs to represent tree stumps. He said this "clearcut" forest was what was left of his life. I saw Samuel several years later and he told me that he woke up one morning, after a year of hard internal work, with a vivid image of a clearcut where a small alder was beginning to grow. "Not a very big one, but before I opened my eyes I saw this small sapling of a tree." Samuel was touched by the vivid immediacy of the image, but had no idea what it meant until his morning commute on the interstate came to a standstill. "All of a sudden I remembered my model from a year ago! All those stumps! Well, an alder is the first thing to start growing in a clearcut. My life was coming back! If I could have gotten out of my car and danced right then and there, I would have."

When Samuel returned home from work, he retrieved his "clearcut" from the basement. He went to a nearby park, collected several alder leaves, and stuck them, outsize, in his clearcut. He sat there with those green leaves and felt something greening deep inside of himself. Samuel began meditating on his landscape every day, and discovered to his delight that, as his outer life shifted and began moving toward a new life of deepened compassion for himself and others, his "forest" began to regrow.

Samuel had taken a middle-management job that had no joy for him, simply to dig himself out of his deep financial hole. "Looking at those green leaves, I realized I had the energy now to do something more with my life than just show up at work." Samuel added a leaf each day to his clearcut, taking away the stumps one by one and replacing them with tiny cedar branches. "Life was coming back, even though I was certain it never would. I started noticing my neighbors, having conversations with people in the grocery checkout lines. I got back to the gym. I started asking myself what I really wanted to do with my life."

I was ushered into Rebirth once by a dream. After more than a year of dealing with the trauma of remembered childhood abuse, I dreamt that I returned home and realized that someone had been in my house.

This someone has left behind a smell almost of roses. I don't feel afraid, as if an intruder had broken in, but rather curious, to see what this Someone may have left behind. I search the house for clues, and get nothing other than the faint, enduring smell of roses, until I go down to the basement, and notice the dryer door slightly ajar. I pull it open and find, to my utter delight, a beautiful baby resting in the warmth of the dryer. I pull it out and know that the baby is mine. It is the most beautiful baby I've ever seen.

Anderson, the artist you met in Chapter Five, had a surprising conversation one evening with her husband, who had been dead for two years. Anderson had frequently conversed with him during her Wilderness time; she wasn't sure if these conversations were "real," but he gave her support and surprisingly good guidance for several years. "Then, one evening," Anderson recalls, "it was like he was *really* there—he felt so present and so alive. He looked at me in a way he did when he'd get frustrated with me—the corners of his mouth would get very tight—and he said to me, 'So listen, Anderson, when are you going to get on with your life?'

"I didn't know what he meant, and told him so. I could almost hear him huffing, and then he said, 'Anderson, start dating. *Get a life.*' Well, I almost fell out of my chair at that one. Friends had been trying to fix me up with someone, but I just wasn't ready. I don't know if that was really my husband or not, but after he told me that, I felt free to reengage with life. I went out on my first date two weeks later."

Cynthia, the woman recovering from rape, had an astonishing thought one Sunday morning in church. When she was a teenager, Cynthia had always dreamed of marrying a minister. "I don't know why, but I would daydream about being a minister's wife, getting to help people at the church. I'd see myself having some status as the minister's wife where I could get a really good teen group going." During a time of quiet prayer during the service on that particular morning, she asked herself a surprising Big Question: Why do I have to go through all the incredible hassle of finding an available man who's a minister, making sure we somehow fall in love with each other, then getting married, so that I can have the life I dreamed of? *Why don't I just eliminate all the in-between stuff and become a minister myself?* Cynthia, who had been raised as a conservative Christian, had never even entertained that option before.

Cynthia felt both excited and overwhelmed—thrilled at the possibility of gifting herself with the life she'd always dreamed of and daunted by what it would take to get there. She talked with her own minister and began to look at practical first steps. "When I'd get overwhelmed at everything I'd have to do, and afraid I couldn't do it, I'd go to the mirror and tell myself, 'Look,

Cynthia. You went through the worst thing that you could ever imagine going through, and you're coming out the other side. Anything else, compared to that, will be a piece of cake. Maybe two years ago you couldn't have done this, but you sure can now.'"

SIGNS OF REBIRTH

Welcome to Rebirth, to New Life. Many of us, during our long sojourn in Wilderness, feel as if New Life will never come. I have felt that way each time I've gone through an initiatory journey. Even though my head *knows* that if I honor the journey, powerful new life will come, it sure doesn't feel that way in my heart. Each time Rebirth comes, I find myself delighted, and amazed anew that this process really does work.

What are some signs of Rebirth?

- You have a dream (like mine of the baby) that signals and symbolizes new life.
- You feel your energy returning, a new spring in your step.
- You regain an interest in your life, in others around you, and in the world.
- An image comes to you, or a question or a daydream, that brings New Life or a new calling.
- You get feedback from others: They notice new color in your face or more energy in your voice.
- There's a deep longing to try something new, move somewhere, do something that piques your interest or stirs your soul.
- A long-buried old dream resurfaces in your life, in its original form or (as with Cynthia above) with a new twist.
- You find yourself looking more now to your future, rather than spending so much time looking back at your past.
- You have a subtle but very real feeling that new life, and new possibili ties, are awaiting you.
- You fall in love: with yourself, a new dream or vocation, or maybe even another person!

Rebirth signals that a deep healing has taken place. For those with life-threatening or chronic illness, Rebirth may not be synonymous with a "cure" or the cessation of physical symptoms. Barbara Fischer, a psychotherapist, struggled with excruciating fibromyalgia for many years before she realized she could be healed into a new life without being cured of her chronic pain.

"Things other than my physical health were reborn instead," Fischer recalls. "I began to have new ideas and find new things that gave me joy. My creativity really began to flourish. I thought of new ways to work instead of just trying harder at the old ways. New ideas came to me, out of my experience of being in Wilderness, that didn't depend upon me recovering my health." Fischer got the idea of offering what she had learned through her experience of illness to others in chronic pain, and her retreats for people in chronic pain were born.

"In Rebirth, a much larger context for my life was now present," says Fischer. "It stopped being about healthy/not healthy; I realized that I had released the old demand to be healthy. It was just too narrow; it didn't work, and all it led to was despair. I began to consider what my soul needed instead, and the very fabric of myself began to reknit in a new way. My actual experience of pain didn't change, but I held the pain in Rebirth in a radically different way because there was a larger context for it. A whole new life emerged when I could just sit and ask my what *soul* needed."

For those with a life-threatening illness, Rebirth doesn't even have to mean staying alive. What it can mean, for those who find themselves dying, is a radically new way of holding their own life and a bittersweet willingness to begin the passage toward physical death.

Dr. Barry Grundland, a psychiatrist who teaches meditation to people with life-threatening illnesses, told me about such a person who experienced Rebirth as he began his journey toward death. John had lymphoma and was finally told he had about two months to live. John invited friends and family to come spend time with him. He asked them before they came to bring something he could take with him on his passage.

"In our culture, we rarely give someone who's dying something to help carry them forward," says Dr. Grundland. "Usually, we spend time with them talking about memories." John's last several months were wonderful. Friends and family brought objects and gifts. Some brought a saying, or a drawing they made. "Other people," recalls Dr. Grundland, "simply brought their breath as a gift. John glowed during this process. It was an extraordinary process, full of grace." When the blessing of his journey was done, John was ready to go, and he died peacefully.

However your Rebirth makes itself known, chances are you'll initially feel vulnerable (often in a wonderful way), tentative, and tender. Think about any new beginning: the first green shoots and fragile buds in spring; the baby-bird-like downy fuzz of post-chemotherapy hair; the sweet openness and vulnerability of babies of any sort, human or otherwise; even the tender pink skin that slowly grows after a serious physical wound.

Beginnings are soft, tender, fragile; this is simply their nature. *This means that your job, as an initiate, is to compassionately hold, and care for, your new self and your emerging new life and dreams.*

TENDING THE SHOOTS

As the gardener of your own life-soil, you'll be tending those tender green shoots of New Life. Here are several suggestions:

• **Don't overdrive your headlights.** Once upon a time I was an impatient young graduate student, chafing at the restrictions of being an intern. My supervisor, Dr. Doug Anderson, one of the world's great wise men, sat me down in his office and asked if I had ever driven a dark mountain road at night. Of course, I answered (impatiently!), wondering when he'd get to the point. He asked me what was the most important thing to remember when driving under those conditions. I went in my imagination to driving Blewett Pass at midnight, and realized how important it was to drive slowly and consciously. "And why is it important to drive slowly?" queried Doug. It seemed like such an obvious question that I became even more impatient as I answered him. "Because I couldn't see past the furthest reach of my headlights if I drove too fast. I couldn't see potential danger, or another driver on a sharp turn, before I had time to react. *"So, it's about not overdriving your headlights?"* Doug asked casually. OH, I thought somewhat sheepishly, I GET IT. I understood that if I were to go "faster" than my training allowed, I could cause some real damage to myself or my clients. Doug's advice applies equally to those who are in the beginning stages of Rebirth. Sometimes it just feels so good to be alive that we want to rush into our New Life. We may be so utterly sick and tired of the not-knowing of Wilderness that we jump at anything for closure, even if it's premature closure. Although we may generate Big Ideas at the beginning of rebirth, it is important to befriend them, mull them over, "sleep" on them to see if they really represent a new direction or just our impulse to get moving. Patience, patience, patience.

• **Take one step at a time.** When new ideas appear, break them down into manageable steps. Often all we get is the first step, like the first clue in a treasure hunt. When Anita, the marketing executive who walked away from her former life, discovered that what she wanted to do was work with nonprofit organizations, she was at a loss for how to proceed, since she had spent her working life immersed in a different world. She asked her-self what the first step might be, if she could imagine just the first tiny step, and she realized it was taking a friend who was the Executive Director of a children's organization out to lunch, to begin learning about the world of nonprofits. One of my all-time favorite movie scenes was from one of the Indiana Jones films. Remember when Harrison Ford finds himself at the edge of a deep canyon where an ancient map tells him that the only way forward is to take a step over the edge of the cliff? Ford, against all better reasoning, steps off into thin air. As soon as he does that, a bridge appears that had been there all along but wasn't visible until his first step. That may happen to us (minus the threat of death, but some-times no less scary!) over and over at the beginning of Rebirth. Remember, all you are being asked to do is take the first step.

• **Don't wait for the Perfect Time to start.** A client in Rebirth brought me a wonderful cartoon several years ago. A man was standing at a cross-roads with signs pointing in two directions. The first sign read "To

Heaven." The second sign read "Workshops on how to get to Heaven." We've all been there. After a divorce, we want to read one more book on dating to make sure we "get it right" before we start. When we've been called to go back to graduate school to begin the career of our dreams, we wonder if it might be better a couple of years from now, when we've got more money, or maybe even in ten years or so, after the kids are out of the house. Sometimes it is important to practice patience, and wait for the right timing. Sometimes, though, it's not about cultivating patience; it's about acknowledging and dealing with our anxieties. Anxiety and fear may simply be telling us we're moving to the creative edge of our own lives, rather than signaling actual danger. Sometimes it's just necessary to feel the fear and move ahead anyway. Spend some time doing internal discernment work to see if it's anxiety that's holding you back rather than prudence. Pray for guidance. Talk with a trusted friend who knows you well, or consult a therapist.

• **Learn to trust the nonrational.** Notice I didn't say the *ir*rational. In Rebirth, we are often guided to think bigger, deeper, and out of our customary box. We are called to pay attention to our daydreams, quick flashes of intuition, gut "knowings," dreams, and synchronicities. We are asked to put the inner critic away for the moment and stretch beyond what we may think is possible for our lives. If we use our everyday minds to entertain new possibilities, chances are we'll get the same answers we've always gotten. It's not exactly "Garbage in, garbage out," but rather "Old business in, old business out." When the idea came out of the blue to Cynthia to enter the ministry, she immediately rejected it. With my encouragement, she allowed herself to sidle back up to the idea, look at it out of the corner of her eye, and play with the possibilities. She allowed the idea to stretch her, rather than demanding that it shrink down to the size of what she already knew. If you are acquainted with any divinatory system, such as the I Ching, the runes, or a Tarot deck, ask for new ideas and play with these. Or, when a new thought comes to you in a dream or flash of intuition, ask the divinatory system of your choice for guidance and feedback. Anderson was tempted to dismiss her deceased husband's advice about getting a life and beginning to date as something she made up. She decided to pull a Tarot card for feedback, and drew "The Fool," stepping happily off a cliff (like Indiana Jones!) into a new adventure and a new life. She put the card on her altar, and it gave her just the courage she needed to call a friend and announce she was ready to date.

• **Know how to recognize a genuine call.** Calls in Rebirth may be a call toward just about anything. Gregg Levoy writes in *Callings*, "Calls may be to do something (become self-employed, go back to school, leave or start a relationship, move to the country, change careers, have a child) or calls to be something (more creative, less judgmental, more loving, less fearful)." Levoy suggests asking these questions for discerning if a call is "true": Does it make you feel more awake, more alive? Is there a sense of rightness to it? Do you find you have surprising tolerance for the mundane tasks involved in its undertaking? Do you feel gratitude for it? Do your friends tell you that they haven't seen you so alive in a long time? Do you, as he writes, "experience gales of resistance (which can indicate the importance of a call)"? True calls keep coming back; they dance in dreams and synchronicities, they give you energy, since they are aligned with your deepest values. They may also be scary; as Levoy notes, often these callings, no matter how large or small, are literally calling you into new territory and New Life. Jason, whose wife left him, recommitted to a high dream of marriage after questioning the institution along with everything else. He realized he wanted to be married to someone who deeply cared about him and was willing to show it, which was something he hadn't experienced with a woman before. This call to be with someone who actively cared about him just about scared the pants off of him, as Jason put it. He realized that in order to move into this dream, he was being called to care about himself at a deeper level than he ever had, and to trust opening up to others and receiving their love in new ways.

If you feel any resistance to the new life being offered you in Rebirth, please know that it's normal. This resistance can show up in any number of ways. You might feel anxious or scared about new possibilities. You might spend a great deal of time and energy telling yourself that your new life, in whatever form it is calling to you, is illogical, unreasonable, or impossible. You might feel that you're being disloyal to someone you love who has died. Any and all of this is part of the process of Rebirth. New Life is, after all, new life. After a lifetime of Somebody Training, to allow ourselves to truly be ourselves, truly claiming our own powerful authenticity, can engender some anxiety. Resisting resistance, however, will only get you more stuck. When you feel resistance in any of its hydra-headed forms, simply acknowledge it, breathe into it, and soften around it. Ask it if it has any new information that is important for you to be aware of, or if it's simply anxiety around the new.

You can lessen your resistance by consciously creating a bridge between your old and your new self. Name the continuities that still remain: Swiss chocolate is still your favorite decadent pleasure; your husband and children have stuck with you through your Wilderness; kayaking, or gardening, or spending an evening with a mystery novel is still your idea of a wonderful time. The more you can acknowledge and honor these continuities between old and new self, the less resistance you'll feel about moving into New Life.

CELEBRATION

In tribal cultures, the whole community celebrates when an initiate returns to them, reborn. They celebrate not only the initiate's return, but the new gifts and visions of the initiate, which will ultimately revitalize and renew the whole community.

The Hero's Journey, Joseph Campbell's model of the journey of all heroes and heroines throughout time and culture, culminates with The Return to his or her original home. Heroes/heroines, however, never come back empty-handed. According to Campbell, they always return with a Boon, a gift gained from the journey to give to the world around them. Carol Pearson, a teacher of the Hero's Journey, writes in *The Hero Within*, "The heroic quest is about saying Yes to yourself and, in so doing, becoming more fully alive and more effective in the world. For the hero's journey is first about taking a journey to find the treasure of your true self, and then about returning home to give your gift to help transform the kingdom—and, in the process, your own life."

As a reborn initiate, as the heroine or hero of your own Quest, you can celebrate your return with the community that has supported your throughout your journey. You can perform a ritual of "reincorporation" into your community that will serve three purposes:

- Thanking your community (whether a community of 2 or 200) for their support
- Allowing your community, and yourself, to name and honor your emergent strengths and gifts
- Celebrating your new life

Anita, the marketing executive turned nonprofit consultant, decided it was time to celebrate when she finished her first consulting job. She asked fifteen of her closest friends and family to bring a small gift, some object representing a newfound gift or strength they saw in her as a result of her journey. She, in turn, bought and found small objects for each of her friends that represented to her the unique gifts they had offered her in support.

They all gathered at Anita's house one evening. Anita opened the circle by thanking each on of them in turn for how they had believed in her and supported her, giving them their gifts and explaining the meaning of each one. Anita gave her sister a tiny china bluebird because, as Anita explained, her sister had kept reminding her that she had a unique song to sing in the world. She gave her best friend a rock engraved with the word "faith," telling her friend that she had indeed been Anita's "rock" for two years, faithfully standing by her in some very dark times.

When she was finished, Anita sat down and received symbolic gifts from each of her guests: a small velvet heart to represent her heart opening, a colored pinwheel for a sweet and playful part of herself that had emerged, a red candle for her new passion for helping others. "It was so challenging for me to stay present in the middle of that much love and caring," recalls Anita, "but it changed my life. I realized how deeply I was loved. I felt like now I could do *anything*, with that kind of backing." The evening culminated in a celebratory potluck.

Gretchen Schodde thanked her community for standing with her through her chemotherapy by having a "Celebration of Life" afternoon at Harmony Hill. Thirty people gathered; one by one they explained how they knew Gretchen, and what they loved about her. Schodde had bought enough materials for everyone to make prayer arrows (compare Interlude Six) for their own gratitudes and dreams, and we all spent a merry afternoon decorating our arrows and celebrating Gretchen's new life. Gretchen asked if everyone would make an additional prayer arrow for future participants at the Harmony Hill Cancer Retreats, since she now had a much more deeply felt understanding of the challenges they faced. The celebration concluded with a basketful of prayer arrows, which were blessed for future retreat participants.

When you are ready, give yourself the immense gift of a community celebration; it's a gift not just for you, but for your support team as well. This event can be as elaborate as Anita's ritual, or simply a potluck or open house in which you get a chance to thank those who have stayed by you and supported you. New Life is truly something to celebrate.

Interlude Ten

CREATING A VISION

By creating this collage, you can engage the more creative side of yourself in envisioning and celebrating Rebirth.

Materials needed: poster board, scissors and glue stick, magazines, glitter/ribbons/crayons/stickers/felt pens (if you wish to decorate with more than magazine images), and favorite music for the background if you wish. Give yourself several hours; this project can be spread over more than one session.

Spread out with your materials at a time when you won't be interrupted. Give yourself a moment to reflect on your journey, all you've learned, where it's taken you. When you're ready, breathe into your heart and ask yourself, "Where is Rebirth taking me? What, and who, is being reborn?" Don't search for answers; this is simply setting the intention for the collage in your heart.

Go through the magazines and tear out any images and words that catch your attention, even if you don't know why. When you are done, cut out your images and words, and play with arranging them on the poster board. Everybody has different ways of collaging; some people like thickly overlapping images, others sparse and simple arrangements. Again, don't give too much thought at this point to what the images "mean." When an arrangement pleases you (don't worry too much about aesthetics), glue the pieces down with the glue stick, and decorate with stickers, glitter, or the like, if you wish. If a word or phrase is important to you, you can either cut the letters out from a magazine, or write them in your own hand and glue them into the collage.

When you are done, prop the poster board up, step back, and take in your creation. How is this a snapshot of your life right now, or your life to come? Look for patterns in the arrangement, clusters of images or words. Are there themes in your collage? If there were a title for this collage, what might it be? If this collage could speak, what might it say to you? Record your responses in your journal. Ask your nondominant hand if there's anything else about this collage that you've missed that's important to know.

If you find particular images jumping out at you, spend some time with them. Ask yourself what attracts, repels, frightens, or excites you about the image; it may carry some important message for you. Let it speak to you through your nondominant hand; ask the image whatever you'd like, and allow your nondominant hand to respond.

After I've made a collage, I like to hang it right beside my bed where I'll see it right before sleep and again first thing in the morning. Collages can be very potent tools both for mirroring the unknown within ourselves and helping us to birth a wonderful and powerful future.

COMMUNITY CELEBRATION

This celebration has three parts: a time for you to thank your community; a time for your community to honor you; and a time to simply celebrate by sharing food. Below are a framework and ideas for such a celebration.

What is most important is that you create a celebration that fits you. Some people go the whole nine yards; others want a simpler celebration, a potluck dinner that includes some words of thanks for their support community. What I have noticed is that most people initially want to pare it down due to discomfort about being the center of that much attention. What many have found, though, is if they push a little through that discomfort and allow themselves to be celebrated and their journey honored, the community celebration turns out to be one of the high points of their life.

Decide on whom you'd like to invite, set a date and time, and ask people to bring something for a potluck celebration at the end. If someone can't be there, you can ask him or her to send a letter, poem, or inspirational quote for you, to be read by someone else at the celebration.

Thanking the community. When all are gathered, thank your community for their support of you in your initiatory journey. Some initiates like to go around the circle and thank each person for specific support; others like to hand out small gifts or tokens of appreciation, one by one, to each person. Other ideas are poems, handmade gifts, or letters of appreciation. Go with what speaks most to your heart about your own gratitude for these people.

Naming your gifts. Ask each participant to bring some token or symbol of a gift or strength he or she has seen emerge in you as a result of your journey— for example, a small rock to represent strength, a heart-shaped sachet for the emergence of new heartfulness, a candle for your new vocational fire. When you are ready, sit in the circle yourself, take a deep breath, and let these people name and appreciate your new gifts. If someone is willing, have him or her be a scribe and write down who gave you what, and what strength or gift each offering represents.

Celebrating. Bring out the food! Food is a wonderful way to ground the expansive energy raised by such a ceremony. Enjoy. You richly deserve it.

11
The Gifts of Homecoming

And so, the end is where we start from. . . . We have reached the final chapter of this book together, you and I, sister and brother journeyers into Mystery.

I have carried this book within me for twenty years, ever since my discovery about initiation and rites of passage ignited a bonfire in my soul. Getting the book published has been a six-year journey of its own. I've fantasized countless times about breezing my way through this final chapter, eager to send the manuscript off to my editor.

I began writing this chapter yesterday morning and discovered how off the mark my fantasy was. I sat slack-jawed and word-empty before my laptop's blank screen, filled with a bittersweet grief to see this part of the journey ending, and feeling completely unworthy to try to write anything worth saying about the ineffable grace of the gifts of initiation. I was reminded of the Zen saying about the uselessness of fingers pointing at the moon: It is the moon, and not the fingers, that we need to see. How very small my "fingers" felt at I watched the blinking cursor, and how utterly luminous the moon of Spirit glowed.

I decided to write to my e-mail support group, friends who have unflaggingly cheered me on, prayed for my writing, and continually reminded of me how wonderful friends can be during such a process. Here is the message I posted:

I'm hitting the first major bump of this writing journey. I'm beginning the last chapter (!!!!), and after looking forward to this for so many years, it's more challenging than I expected. The bump is that, in writing this last chapter, I'm also writing the "last chapter" in a phase of my life that has lasted almost twenty years, namely the dream of writing this book! As I sit here writing this message to you, as I avoid staring at the blank screen of what will be Chapter 11, the journey of the last several decades is playing out in my heart. I feel more than a little overwhelmed, with a good dollop of bittersweet grief over this leg of the journey coming to an end.

I'm needing faith in myself to say what I know deep inside about the gifts of the initiatory journey: compassion, wisdom, and reverence for life. Connecting my heart with my voice about such things is such a huge challenge for me sometimes. I've got a touch of what my best friend in high school called the "lowly wormies" (after we studied the Psalms in English class): Who am I (there's the lowly worm!) to try and articulate such things? I'm laughing about it, but it's real, this wondering whether I have the ability to talk about that which is truly unnameable and holy.

Please send your prayers my way this week for confidence to lean into the stiff headwinds of finishing the book. Thank you so much for your help.

My friend Lu responded immediately:

It sounds as though you are living the book, including the grieving, loss, growth and transformation. I picture you as a butterfly emerging from your cocoon with all the struggle and joy inherent in that journey. My prayers for your heart to remain open and the winds of heaven to lift your wings are with you. You are truly writing about sacred events and holy places. I wonder if the place to start is just to acknowledge the ineffability of such things, then see where your writing goes from there.

So here I am following Lu's advice. My heart is open, and full of the journey we're all on. My words really are nothing but fingers pointing at the sweet full Moon of love and spirit. I hope they point you in the right direction.

Welcome to the world of the initiated. Just as Jacob became Israel in the story in Chapter One, and limped for the rest of his life from the shattering of his thigh by the angel, so too has your soul been marked by your trauma. You will forever bear the scar of this wounding. For some of you, the scar will recede over time to a small stitch in your soul-skin, which will remind you of this initiatory journey from time to time. For others, as in the death of a child, the scar may never totally recede, and may ache and throb—as old wounds often do—during the weather changes of your life.

Whether your arrival here has taken you months or years, you are now beginning to experience the fruits of your wounding as well. As in all initiations, these fruits are meant to be shared and celebrated with the world around you.

"When initiations are successful, the survivors slowly return to their communities with new eyes to see, new ears to hear, and the courage to act upon these perceptions," writes Kat Duff, a survivor of chronic fatigue syndrome, in *The Alchemy of Illness*. Tribal initiations were enacted, not simply for the transformation of the individual but for the transformation and renewal of the community. And so it is with you. You have traveled the same road as the ancient tribal initiates, braved challenges just as severe, and returned, just as they did, with new life and new gifts.

Remember, oh so long ago at the beginning of your initiatory journey, naming your "dis" words? Disengagement, Disidentification, Disillusionment, Disorientation, and Disintegration. I had told you that Dis was another name for Pluto, the Roman God of the Underworld. Romans believed that the Underworld was the ultimate source of wealth; though it was dark and terrifying, rubies, riches, and gold all issued from its mysterious depths. I promised you in Chapter Two that if you honored your trauma as the beginning of an initiatory journey, you would get to mine its secret riches and create a new and transformed life with them. You have made your initiatory journey through grief and loss, and now return carrying that wealth in your heart and soul.

These riches fall into four broad categories: new individual gifts, strengths, and callings; heightened compassion for self and others; wisdom; and a deeper reverence for life.

NEW GIFTS

"Each of us, as we journey through life, has the opportunity to find and to give his or her unique gift(s)," writes Jungian analyst Helen Luke, in

An African Tale. "Whether that gift is great or small in the eyes of the world does not matter at all—not at all. It is through the finding and the giving that we may come to know the joy that lies at the center of both the dark times and the light."

You have journeyed, and found your gifts. As Luke says, the size of those gifts matters not a whit. What does matter is your naming and claiming of them. While for some their gifts may be dramatic or visibly larger, for others theirs may look "insignificant" in the eyes of our culture.

Gretchen Schodde recognized that her heart and soul (and body) really didn't belong behind a desk as an administrator. "In order to keep going as Executive Director, I realized I needed to get back out to the gardens at Harmony Hill, which I had left behind because everything else at Harmony Hill seemed too all-consuming and important. After the cancer, I realized that gardening was as necessary for me as breathing." Gretchen was inspired by the yoga classes at the cancer retreats, but when she realized that she needed something outdoors, she invented her own form of yoga. When a garden labyrinth at Harmony Hill was threatened with being plowed under due to lack of available help, Gretchen decided to adopt the garden maintenance of the labyrinth as her own yoga. YOLL, she calls it: Yoga of the Lavender Labyrinth.

One of the greatest gifts I received from my two years in the "underworld" with chronic fatigue syndrome was a heightened awareness of my own mortality. If someone had told me before I fell ill that the sense of my own future death walking every day beside me was a gift, I would have dismissed these words as morose and morbid. My illness, though, gifted me with the daily awareness that this could be my last day on earth. This gift wasn't morbid; it didn't involve brooding over death or being paralyzed with anxiety about when it might happen. Rather, the powerful sense of my own death walking right beside me freed me up to take risks I might never have taken: to say "I love you" more often to friends and family, or to stop in the middle of any activity and treat myself to the beauty of this sweet earth.

With the claiming—or the reclamation—of these gifts comes also a newfound sense of personal power. Not the clenching-our-teeth to make something happen power, not the bending-others-to-our-will kind of power, but the power that comes from deep within, that springs from our newfound depth and passion for life. "What is the source of this soul power, and how can we tap into it?" asks Thomas Moore in *Care of the Soul*. "It comes first of all from living close to the heart, and not at odds with it. Therefore, paradoxically, soul power may emerge from failure, depression, and loss."

The failure, depression, and loss forcibly remove us from Somebody Training and, in the process, leave us with our true Self. Free of having to be Somebody, we can be who we were created to be, with our own unique gifts and strengths, fueled and fed with our own ever-renewing source of soul power.

This soul power is yours; it is a gift of your journey. No one, and nothing, can take it away from you. You'll find that it only grows in strength as you bring your newfound gifts out into the world.

COMPASSION

One day a woman came to the Buddha for guidance about what to do with her inconsolable grief over the loss of her baby. The Buddha advised her to bring back a mustard seed from a house that had never known death. She traveled for days, from village to village; but every household, she discovered, had been visited by death. The woman went back to her own village, buried her child, and then returned to the Buddha.

"Where is your mustard seed?" asked the Buddha.

"Oh, awakened One, I found no such seed," replied the woman. "I learned that everything changes. Everything that is born, dies. No one escapes suffering."

This woman discovered, as any initiate discovers, that we're all in this together. "A heart broken open can contain the whole world," Mother Meera, a Hindu saint, tells us. Trauma breaks our hearts, and the initiatory process teaches us how to keep that broken heart soft and wide open, rather than shutting down in grief and pain.

"Giving and helping others has become a very big part of my healing process," says Diane Nares, the mother of Emilio, who died from leukemia. "I speak with other families whose options are narrowing for their children. I seek knowledge and information about the current world of pediatric cancer. What cures are in the works? Who is doing what research? My husband and I recently returned from Fred Hutchinson Hospital in Seattle, visiting a family whom we had befriended while Emilio was in the hospital. The awareness and concern just keeps us going." Diane and her husband Richard recently started the Emilio Nares Foundation, helping families dealing with the challenges of cancer. "I see our work as a direct result of our loss," says Diane. "Through this work we will be honoring Emilio's life, serving others, and continuing to heal ourselves." Diane knows that Emilio is still with her as she reaches out to help others who are suffering just as she and her child suffered: "Everything that we do is inspired by Emilio. He gives us courage and strength."

Compassion literally means "suffering with." It is both a feeling, an opening of the heart toward our own or others' suffering, and an action. Compassion-in-action is foundational to every spiritual path. Indeed, many find that practicing compassion-in-action as a spiritual discipline goes further toward transforming their spiritual life than of prayer or meditation.

Your broken-open, wide-awake, post-initiation heart is perhaps the finest gift you have to offer both yourself and the world around you. I have found, both personally and through working with others, that learning to extend compassion to ourselves when we are feeling broken is one of the biggest challenges of the initiatory process. I remember how astonished I felt when, several decades ago, I read Jesus's admonition to "Love your neighbor as yourself," and finally understood the "as yourself" part for the first time. I asked myself, "What if I treated others as badly as I treated myself? What if I said the same things to others that I said to myself when I looked in the mirror first thing in the morning?" Then, as the weeks passed, I saw to my further astonishment that I *did* treat others as I treated myself. Those days when I particularly beat up on myself were the same days I was particularly critical of friends and strangers alike, the same days I cursed at the car cutting ahead of me in traffic. The days I could extend compassion toward myself usually turned out to be the same days I was aware of how deeply grateful I was to those around me and told them so, the same days I invited a harried mother with an over-the-edge child to step in front of me in the grocery line. Learning to extend compassion to ourselves when we are broken is the finest training we can receive for learning to extend compassion to others in a broken world.

Jason, whose wife left him, first heard about the Big Brother program (a nationwide volunteer program that matches up men with boys needing a positive male presence in their lives) while married. "It sounded interesting. I sure could have used it when I was a kid, but I didn't want to think about that any more. I just wanted to be married, enjoy my job, get on with my life." Jason's perspective on his and others' pain radically changed after his divorce.

"In that year, I think I learned for the first time to be kind to myself, especially when I was in pain. That led me to thinking about all those boys out there without dads. Since I wasn't dodging my own pain any more, I could let theirs in." When Jason's energy for life returned at Rebirth he became a Big Brother. He found to his surprise that connecting with a boy on a weekly basis turned out to be the biggest gift of his divorce. "Her leaving devastated me. It stopped me short in my tracks. I just couldn't keep moving through my life the way I had been doing. When I stopped, I had to really pay attention for the first time in my life to my own pain. Her leaving me that way, that kind of betrayal, made me realize how many kids were getting betrayed in the same way, and I wanted to do something about that."

Where does your broken-open heart take you? Where might you extend to others the same love and compassion you are learning to extend to yourself? You might find yourself being drawn to do some volunteer work like Diane and Jason. You may simply make a decision to be kinder to other drivers on your morning commute, or offer to help a neighbor with babysitting. I have included instructions for the rest of Metta, the Buddhist self-compassion practice you learned in Chapter Three, in the Interlude at the end of this chapter. Given how deeply connected we all are, all of us, practicing Metta can be one of the most powerful things you can ever do to offer love and compassion to others.

WISDOM

The big difference between knowledge and wisdom, someone once told me, is that knowledge helps you make a living, while wisdom helps you make a life. Wisdom—totally neglected in our speeded-up culture, desperately needed in our foundering world—is one of initiation's greatest gifts.

We are not born with wisdom. Wisdom only comes from living, and usually is gleaned more deeply during trying times. Wisdom is gained by making mistakes and suffering deeply and healing. Going through initiation is like enrolling in Wisdom School at the graduate level.

The wisdom gained from the initiatory journey is threefold: the awareness of the Big Picture, the ability to let go, and the capacity to live a life full of meaning.

- **Big Picture.** "What may feel like a tragic accident or illness at one level may be the catalyst—perhaps even a call—for a deeper and more meaningful soul-self," writes Robert Keck, who has dealt with the pain of post-polio syndrome all of his adult life. In *Healing as a Sacred Path*, he writes, "In other words, what our current identity, our primary personality, and our style of life may consider to be a major problem could very well be the soul's process of change, growth, and development." Keck arrived at his Big Picture after years of dealing with his own pain, disability, and healing. Coming to your own place of understanding how your own trauma fits into the Big Picture, how it has been the catalyst for a more meaningful life, may take you many years as well. Celebrate it when you get there. This is the deepest sort of wisdom, this Mystery that comes out of tragedy; it will allow your New Life to flower abundantly.

- **Ability to let go.** "Everything I've ever let go of has had my claw marks all over it," someone said once. Over the years, I've had to let go of different things that I've thought I *had* to have for a good life: health, marriage, abundant IRAs. Deep inside, I was terrified that somehow my life would end. It did, and I discovered, time after time, that there was life after metaphorical death. I'm a slow learner, but I've managed to finally get the Budhha's teaching about impermanence: Everything, and everyone, passes away, including myself. No exceptions. What I've discovered in learning to let go is that, for almost everything I've let go of, something else even better has taken its place.

• **A life of meaning.** Carl Jung reflected in his later years that life was meant not for the pursuit of happiness, but for the search for meaning. Happiness, he said, is a fruitless goal because it is by its nature transient. Meaning, however, stays with us and gives life a powerful richness and depth. Trauma and initiation invite us into a life devoted to meaning. One of the gifts, ironically, of the successful search for meaning is a deep and simple happiness. (It rarely works the other way, that the pursuit of happiness brings a life of depth and meaning.) When we can harvest meaning from trauma, we open our soul's door wide to joy. Happiness tends to be connected to "stuff": a relationship, a day off, a new TV. Joy is wilder, wider, and essentially untamable; it opens the heart and frees the spirit. Joy follows closely on the heels of meaning. When I reap and celebrate the gifts of my initiatory process, I discover a deeper meaning there, a life of connection and passion rather than one of superficial adjustment. "When you truly possess all that you have been and done," wrote octogenarian Florida Scott Maxwell in *The Measure of My Days*, "which may take some time, you are fierce with reality." Finding a deeper meaning through your initiatory passage will leave you fierce with reality and alight with joy.

The wisdom gained during the initiatory process empowers us to seek, and live, not a perfect life, but a life that is full, rich, embodied, and soulful.

REVERENCE FOR THE SACREDNESS OF LIFE

"Initiation improves your spiritual life tremendously," says Barbara Fischer. "The encounter with the Sacred can truly happen, in a very real way, after trauma. Trauma breaks us wide open; it creates room to be touched, to be engaged, by something bigger than yourself. After such an initiation, our relationship to life itself is never the same."

All of the challenges and trials of initiation wear away our resistance to simply being, and receiving, Life. I am reminded of the apocryphal story in which someone asked Michelangelo how he created such glorious masterpieces as the Pieta. Michelangelo replied that it was simple, really; all he did was chip away everything that wasn't the statue.

Initiation is like Michelangelo's hammer and chisel. It not only removes anything that is not really us, it also chips away all familial and cultural blinders to the immense and utterly inexplicable beauty and sacredness of life itself. When we drop out of the rat race, we reconnect to the simple and extraordinary presence of the Sacred within our own heart and souls, in our relationships, in the limitless expressions of God in the world around us. We can behold, and experience, love and miracles unfolding in the most mundane details of everyday life.

"I think—no, I *know*—that I took everything for granted a whole lot of the time," reflects Marge, the breast cancer survivor you met in Chapter Three. "A home, a husband, good kids, satisfying work—looking back on that pre-mastectomy me. But I was just sleepwalking through a whole lot of that. When I really looked death in the face and saw that all of my life could just go in a second, I woke up. That's it: I woke up! *No more sleepwalking through life.* I know that means waking up to everything, not just the roses. It means being awake, really awake, for the pain as well as the joy. I understand now that it's a package deal: the awful stuff as well as the great."

The good news is, though, that this package deal comes with an unconditional guarantee: that if you "do the program," your capacity for unbridled joy, deep wisdom, and a grateful reverence for Spirit and all the gifts of life will fill you beyond your wildest imaginings.

With initiation you were enrolled in The School of Fierce Reality, and you then dropped out of Somebody Training. You have found the treasure of your true self. The post-Somebody Training, broken-open Self is wired into a larger reality, that Life which is beyond suffering, destruction, and change. This Self, which is now chiseled free of all that was not-self, is more fully connected to life and love, and this Self is gifted with a deep inner knowing of what really counts as we journey through the rest of our life. According to Jeanne Achterberg, we have remembered what was forgotten, embraced what was feared, opened what was closed, and softened what had been hardened. We have healed into who we really are, which opens us to the ineffable gift of receiving Life as it really is.

YOUR HOMECOMING WILL BE MY HOMECOMING

"Your homecoming will be my homecoming," writes poet e. e. cummings. At some very deep and inexplicable level, we are all connected, filaments from heart to heart humming below all the contemporary cacophony of phones, stereos, and freeway noise. Tribal cultures knew this and celebrated that the ultimate purpose of initiation was not only self-renewal, but the ensuing renewal of the community, flowing from the initiate's rebirth.

We are all born with a great Homesickness, and spend much of our lives self-medicating that longing for the Beloved through work, relationships, retail therapy, and television. Initiation carries us Home, right into the arms of the Beloved.

A question I am frequently asked is, "Now that I've done this journey, can I be sure that I will never have to do it again?" I always have to truthfully answer, "No." Being initiated does not inoculate us from further trauma.

However, you now know not just the map but the territory itself. "Going through the death and rebirth of initiation gives us confidence in the cycles of life," explains Barbara Fischer. "You learn that what looks like death ain't necessarily so. It may look and feel and taste like death, but you learn that something is always being born out of that death, something entirely new. To really experience initiation and move through to Rebirth gives you great faith that you will be able to deal with whatever else life may throw at you. You don't dread the next time you'll encounter some god-awful loss, or wonder if you'll be able to cope with it; you'll know, from experience, that more comes from initiation than you lose."

I once spent an evening at Rancho la Puerta listening to Bill, the head gardener of their prized organic gardens, speak with the sweet southern drawl of his Texas farm boyhood about his love for tending the soil. A woman raised her hand and apologized that, due to his accent, she couldn't tell if he was speaking with so much joy about "soil" or "soul."

Bill's face lit up, and he said with a smile that it didn't really matter, they were just about the same thing. He then shared with us that, to him, the most important ingredient for the gorgeous vegetables and fruits they grew (and we gratefully ate!) was to feed the soil/soul good compost.

The initiation process is the finest compost there is for growing New Life in your soil/soul. A post-initiation life, as T. S. Eliot wrote in his *Four Quartets*, is "A life of significant soil." This composting process ensures that whatever now grows from your soil/soul will flourish green, lush, and strong.

May you enjoy the bountiful harvest of your composted trauma. May the world around you relish the richness of your life of significant soil. May we all be fed, and healed, by your courage, your gifts, and your New Life.

Interlude Eleven

JOURNAL: HARVESTING MEANING

William Bridges, in *The Way of Transition*, suggests looking at a life transition as a course in the School of Life. Below are two of his questions for harvesting meaning, together with a question of my own. With these questions, I am reminded that the great philosopher Kierkegaard once said that life must be lived forward, but understood backward. Remember that this understanding, and harvesting, will continue for years after your initiatory journey is finished.

The first two questions are Bridges' (paraphrased); the third one is my own.

1. If your initiatory journey were a course in the School of Life, what might the title and subject of that course be?
2. What were the biggest things you had to unlearn? (Think back now, with a little more perspective, to the "dis" words of Chapter Two, as well as anything you subsequently had to unlearn.)
3. If you were to recast your initiatory journey as The Hero's or Heroine's Journey, what was the purpose of your journey? What dragons did you have to slay? What did you learn? What Boon(s) did you return with for the renewal of the world around you?

FULL METTA (LOVING-KINDNESS) MEDITATION

You learned to extend lovingkindess to yourself through the Buddhist Metta meditation in the Interlude for Chapter Three. You may have chosen your own words of compassion, or used the ones I suggested:

May I be at peace.
May I be free from suffering.
May I be healed.
May I know the light of my own true nature.

Now you can learn to extend the same powerful loving-kindness, the fruit of your own initiatory journey, to the world around you. When you are ready, inhale deeply and then release, emptying yourself. If you wish, you may touch your heart lightly to bring your awareness there. Then first repeat to yourself, out loud or silently (using your language, or mine) Metta for yourself:

May I be at peace.
May I be free from suffering.
May I be healed.
May I know the light of my own true nature.

Now bring to heart and mind someone you deeply care about. Offer him or her Metta:

May you be at peace.
May you be free from suffering.
May you be healed.
May you know the light of your own true nature.

Extend Metta now to a friend. After that, extend Metta to someone you feel neutral about: the postman, the neighbor down the street.

When you have finished the "neutral" Metta, it is time to move into more challenging territory. Think now of someone you dislike, someone who irritates you, someone who has hurt you, someone with whom you deeply disagree. (I suggest starting with a "one-pound dislike"—the driver who cut in front of you this morning, a coworker who made a mildly offensive remark. Save the ten- and twenty-pound dislikes—your ex, a parent who deeply wounded you—for later when your "Metta muscles" are in good working order.)

When you have finished with your dislike, move to all beings. You can start with a particular group, such as an endangered species, the inhabitants of Afghanistan, or all those suffering from cancer, or you can simply extend Metta to all who share this planet with you.

If you wish, in closing, offer all benefits accrued from your practice for the healing of all beings everywhere.

Appendix

FOR PARTNERS AND FAMILY

Please know that if you are the partner, family member, or dear friend of someone undergoing initiation, then you are undergoing an initiation of sorts as well. According to an old African saying, "When the initiate fasts, the whole village starves."

Watching someone you dearly love go through the process of initiation can sometimes be as hard as going through it yourself. While the initiate is deeply engrossed in his or her journey, you are left to endure the pain you feel over seeing the person you love suffer. Your feel helpless to lift that suffering, but at the same time you try to support your loved one, and you cultivate deep patience by waiting for his or her New Life to emerge. Your primary tasks are twofold: offer support appropriate to the stage of your loved one's journey, and find support for yourself.

APPROPRIATE SUPPORT

Appropriate is the key word here. Many of us, when trying to support an initiate, go to one of two extremes:

- We may try too hard to support the person, moving in too close when the initiate really needs space, offering too much advice, or fluttering around him or her, trying to figure out what to do. When we try too hard, it is important to recognize that we are doing it not just out of concern for our loved one, but as a way of managing our own anxiety and helplessness over the situation.

•We may withdraw because we feel discouraged and overwhelmed. Withdrawal can take many forms: physical, emotional, or a much more subtle energetic withdrawal, in which our bodies are present but not much else is. Again, it is important to recognize that we withdraw, both because we care so much and as a way to manage our own fears and anxieties.

The magic words for supporting someone in the throes of initiation are in the form of a question: "How can I best support you right now?" Sometimes your loved one will be able to articulate what is needed. At other times, the initiate will feel just as confused about what he or she needs from you as about everything else.

When your loved one is in a relatively clear space, sit down with him or her and find out what sorts of actions generally feel most supportive. Some of us love to be touched; for others, touch is anathema when we feel stressed and overwhelmed. Other possibilities are talking, doing chores and offering practical assistance, cooking and cleaning, or simply being together in silence. If you put together a list of possibilities, you can go down the list with your loved one when he or she doesn't have a clue. Here are some other suggestions of ways to support your loved one:

EMOTIONAL
- Check in and ask how he or she is feeling.
- Offer a neck, hand, or foot massage.
- Support your loved one in taking time for self-care and retreat.
- Sit in quiet support while he or she makes a difficult phone call or does a difficult thing; then offer debriefing time afterward.
- Encourage the initiate to seek professional support when needed.
- Allow your loved one to be in a not-knowing space, without pressuring him or her to figure things out.

- Support the initiate in trusting his or her own timing and taking the time it takes to move through initiation.
- When you see subtle signs of new life, let your loved one know.
- Offer support when your loved one tries something new.

PRACTICAL
- Offer rides to the doctor, and accompany the initiate on medical appointments.
- Help with practical chores, errands, and child care, or find others to do so.
- Field calls and e-mail from the outside world.
- Establish an e-mail support system for the initiate.
- Help your loved one think through decisions that need to be made.
- Help your loved one identify options and articulate pros and cons, without advocating for one in particular.
- Ask questions the initiate might not think of.
- Help clean out closets when the initiate is ready to clear out the "old."
- Listen noncritically when your loved one begins to dream new dreams for his or her life; articulate any patterns and connections you see.
- Help break down new dreams into manageable steps.
- If the initiate seems to be prematurely rushing into a new dream, give him or her feedback, and extend permission to slow down and really think things through.

Watching someone you love suffer is perhaps one of the most difficult things you'll ever have to do. When you're feeling especially helpless and over-whelmed, remember to up your own self-care and compassion. Reread Chapter Seven on letting go; you will often have to do as much letting go and surrendering as your loved one.

There is one final thing you can always do for your loved one at any time: pray. Incontrovertible scientific evidence is mounting that prayer actually does make a difference on all levels, from physical to spiritual. The experiments are reassuring, in that all forms of prayer have been used "successfully." The most important ingredients are your intention for the other person's healing, and your love.

Remember, you are in your own initiation of sorts. Depending upon how much your life is intertwined with the initiate's, you may be experiencing the death of some of your own cherished beliefs and dreams. If this holds true for you, reread this book with yourself in mind, and work with what applies to your own life.

You're doing double-duty right now: Your loved one needs more support now than perhaps you've ever given, at a time when you're perhaps feeling more stressed yourself than you ever have. I offer support people an awkward, but fitting, analogy: Your care for your loved one is like an energy savings account in your name. Whenever you support the initiate, a withdrawal of energy occurs. Remember, you are the only one who can make deposits in your account, through self-care and receiving your own support. As your energy savings account dwindles, so will your capacity to support the initiate. By taking care of yourself (especially during an extended time when that might seem terribly selfish), you increase your ability to compassionately care for the one you love.

Seek support for yourself. If your loved one has a serious illness, find a support group for support persons of people with that illness (the Internet is a good place to search). Find supportive literature for caregivers, and read it. Talk with others who have been through the same experience; they are quite often the best support. When they tell you they understand how hard it is to be in your position, they mean it. Set up a care team of your own, and allow yourself the luxury of leaning on them when necessary. Write up your own self-care list; when your loved one needs space, or is unavailable to you emotionally, go to your list and do something for yourself.

This is your opportunity to discover a new depth of resiliency within yourself. I have had support people tell me that their loved one's initiation provided them with the very important gift of realizing how strong they were. After the initiation they found they were much less afraid of trying new things, and they did not sweat the small stuff anymore. This is your opportunity to receive these same gifts as well as a new depth of spiritual life. Care for yourself, and reap your greatly deserved new life.

Annotated Bibliography

LIFE TRANSITIONS

Bridges, William. *The Way of Transition: Embracing Life's Most Difficult Moments*. Chicago: Perseus Publishing, 2001. Written after the death of Bridges' wife from breast cancer, this honest, beautifully written, and moving book chronicles Bridges' journey through the three stages of transition.

Bridges, William. *Transitions: Making Sense of Life's Changes*. New York: Addison-Wesley, 1980. Well-written, easy-to-read book on the three stages of a life transition.

Heckler, Richard. *Crossings: Everyday People, Unexpected Events, and Life-Affirming Change*. New York: Harcourt Brace & Co., 1998. Heckler looks at the power of unexpected events to transform our lives, giving us a new way of perceiving ourselves in the world.

PRAYER

Dossey, Larry, M.D. *Prayer Is Good Medicine*. New York: HarperCollins, 1997. The standard work on a solid scientific look at prayer. The book is divided into four sections: the scientific evidence for prayer, controversies around prayer experiments, what prayer is, and how to pray.

Manzi, Carolyn. *Coloring Your Prayers: An Inspirational Coloring Book for Making Dreams Come True*. New York: Harmony Books, 2000. Remember how fun it was as a child to curl up with crayons and a coloring book? Manzi has created a whimsical and delightful coloring book for adults on, of all things, prayer. The illustrations to be colored are wonderful and are accompanied by reflections about prayer.

GUIDED IMAGERY

Achterberg, Jeanne, Barbara Dossey, and Leslie Kolkmeier. *Rituals for Healing: Using Imagery for Health and Wellness*. New York: Bantam New Age Books, 1994. This classic on using guided imagery to promote health and wellness offers wonderful guided imagery scripts.

Adair, Margo. *Meditations on Everything under the Sun: The Dance of Imagination, Intuition, and Mindfulness*. Philadelphia: New Society Publishers, 2001. One hundred and sixty meditations/guided imagery scripts address almost every issue that we face in contemporary life. The scripts are ingeniously designed to allow readers to mix and match them to fill their own particular needs.

Naparstek, Belleruth. *Staying Well with Guided Imagery: How to Harness the Power of Your Imagination for Health and Healing*. New York: Warner Books, 1994. Naparstek shows how to use deliberate, directed daydreaming and guided sensory imagery for emotional healing and physical health.

DREAMS

Barasch, Marc Ian. *Healing Dreams: Exploring the Dreams That Can Transform Your Life*. New York: Riverhead Books, 2000. An entire book on Big Dreams: how to work with them, different categories, how different cultures see and work with them. Explores in detail healing dreams, dreams of personal calling, dreams of illness and healing, shadow dreams, communal dreams, and Otherworld dreams.

Moss, Robert. *Conscious Dreaming: A Spiritual Path for Everyday Life*. New York: Three Rivers Press, 1996. Moss presents a unique nine-step approach to understanding dreams, using contemporary dreamwork techniques, influenced by shamanic cultures around the world.

Taylor, Jeremy. *Where People Fly and Water Runs Uphill*. New York: Warner Books, 1993. Wonderful book to help you look more deeply into your own dreaming experience and uncover the multiple meanings behind each dream.

PAIN, FEAR, AND LOSS

Bloomfield, Harold, Melba Colgrove, and Peter McWilliams. *How to Survive the Loss of a Love*. Los Angeles: Prelude Press, 1993. One of the most helpful books on loss ever written, this easy-to-read classic offers comfort, inspiration, and practical ways to deal with loss.

Brehony, Kathleeen. *After the Darkest Hour: How Suffering Begins the Journey to Wisdom*. New York: Henry Holt and Company, 2000. In this thoughtful book, Brehony reveals the transformative power of suffering and shows how to turn grief into opportunities for growth, renewal, and wisdom.

Chodron, Pema. *When Things Fall Apart: Heart Advice for Difficult Times*. Boston: Shambhala Publications, 2000. Drawn from traditional Buddhist teachings (but not just for Buddhists), this book shows how to move toward painful situations with compassion and how to use painful emotions to cultivate wisdom, compassion, and courage. See also her latest book, *The Places That Scare You: A Guide to Fearlessness in Difficult Times* (Shambhala, 2001).

Cohen, Darlene. *Finding a Joyful Life in the Heart of Pain*. Boston: Shambhala Publications, 2000. Subtitled "A Meditative Approach to Living with Physical, Emotional, or Spiritual Suffering," this book is birthed from Cohen's experience as a Zen teacher and a decades-long suffererer of rheumatoid arthritis. With stories, exercises, and a deep awareness from long spiritual practice, she demonstrates how to live with joy in the midst of pain, physical or otherwise.

NEW LIFE

Beck, Martha. *Finding Your Own North Star: Claiming the Life You Were Meant to Live*. New York: Crown Publishers, 2001. A step-by-step program that shows you how to fulfill your deepest potential and repair unconscious beliefs that block you from that fulfillment. A smart, wise, and very funny book.

Levoy, Gregg. *Callings: Finding and Following an Authentic Life*. New York: Harmony Books, 1997. This book is a passionate look at the search for authenticity and a practical inquiry into how we listen and respond to our calls.

MISCELLANEOUS

Harris, Rachel. *20-Minute Retreats: Revive Your Spirits in Just Minutes a Day with Simple Self-Led Exercises*. New York: Henry Holt and Company, 2000. A simple and inspirational book filled with ideas for "retreats" lasting anywhere from one minute to twenty, based on twelve universal themes such as Faith, Healing, and Self-Care.

Lane, Mary Rockwood, R.N., M.S.N., and Michael Samuels, M.D. *Creative Healing: How to Heal Yourself by Tapping Your Hidden Creativity*. San Francisco: HarperSanFrancisco, 1998. Presents readers with inspiring ways in which the arts (painting, writing, music, and dance) can free the spirit to heal. Powerful resource for those who want to use the creative arts to make positive changes in their lives and engage their souls in the healing journey.

Linn, Denise. *Quest: A Guide for Creating Your Own Vision Quest*. New York: Ballantine Books, 1997. This guidebook gives you the necessary tools to create your own vision quest with confidence and safety, whether it's overnight in a cabin or a week in the wilderness. Includes a list of organizations that provide guided vision quests.

Linn, Denise. *Altars: Bringing Sacred Shrines into Your Everyday Life*. New York: Ballantine Books, 1999. Excellent reference on how to create and maintain many different kinds of altars. Great photos of different altars will give lots of ideas.

Markova, Dawna. *I Will Not Die an Unlived Life: Reclaiming Purpose and Passion*. Berkeley: Conari Press, 2000. In these turbulent times of profound uncertainty, nothing is more important than learning the skills of navigating our lives from the inside out. This is an inspiring and beautifully written book on how to awaken a fierce commitment to live life open-heartedly, no matter what comes our way.

Pollack, Rachel. *The Power of Ritual*. New York: Dell Books, 2000. This is a good guidebook for learning simple ways to bring ritual into your life and learning how to create sacred spaces in your home.

West, Melissa. *Exploring the Labyrinth: A Guide for Healing and Spiritual Growth*. New York: Broadway Books, 2000. Inspiring and practical book on how to use one of the oldest contemplative and transformational tools known to humankind. Includes chapters on walking the labyrinth for soothing the spirit, healing, community building, creativity enhancement, and marking important living events.

About the Author

Melissa West, M.S., is nationally known for her groundbreaking work in helping people in profound life transitions. She is Program Director at the Harmony Hill Retreat Center, where she helps facilitate retreats for people with life-threatening illnesses; the co-founder of LifeQuest Institute, an organization devoted to contemporary life transitions and rituals; core faculty in Bastyr University's Spirituality, Health, and Medicine Program; and a psychotherapist and spiritual counselor in Seattle, Washington. Her previous books include *Exploring the Labyrinth: A Guide for Healing and Spiritual Growth* and *If Only I Were a Better Mother*, and she was a coeditor for *Soulful Living: The Process of Personal Transformation*. She lives in Seattle with her daughter and cat.

For more information on Melissa West's work and her workshop and speaking schedule, visit her Web site at www.wisdomways.org, or write her at Melissa@wisdomways.org.